Reaktion's Botanical series is the first of its kind, integrating horticultural and botanical writing with a broader account of the cultural and social impact of trees, plants and flowers.

Published
Apple Marcia Reiss
Ash Edward Parker
Bamboo Susanne Lucas
Berries Victoria Dickenson
Birch Anna Lewington
Cactus Dan Torre
Cannabis Chris Duvall
Carnation Twigs Way
Carnivorous Plants Dan Torre
Cherry Constance L. Kirker and Mary Newman
Chrysanthemum Twigs Way
Geranium Kasia Boddy
Grasses Stephen A. Harris
House Plants Mike Maunder
Lily Marcia Reiss
Mulberry Peter Coles
Oak Peter Young
Orchid Dan Torre
Palm Fred Gray
Pine Laura Mason
Poppy Andrew Lack
Primrose Elizabeth Lawson
Rhododendron Richard Milne
Rose Catherine Horwood
Rowan Oliver Southall
Snowdrop Gail Harland
Sunflowers Stephen A. Harris
Tulip Celia Fisher
Weeds Nina Edwards
Willow Alison Syme
Yew Fred Hageneder

YEW

Fred Hageneder

REAKTION BOOKS

Published by
REAKTION BOOKS LTD
Unit 32, Waterside
44–48 Wharf Road
London N1 7UX, UK

www.reaktionbooks.co.uk

First published 2013
Paperback edition first published 2023
Copyright © Fred Hageneder 2013

Printed and bound in India by Replika Press Pvt. Ltd

A catalogue record for this book is available from the British Library

ISBN 978 1 78914 721 6

Contents

Ancient yew in northern Spain.

Introduction

꙳

Many people today do not know what a yew looks like. Yews do not stand out. They do not grow to towering heights, and do not undergo a transformation from bare to fresh green leaves in spring, or have fire-coloured autumn foliage. Yews do not rustle in the wind, but are silent and non-imposing. They appear as small to medium-sized, dark and inconspicuous woody plants that are commonly found in the corner of a garden or park (often enough the dark corner where people hide the compost heap or rubbish bin). In woodland they grow as part of the understorey – in Europe they occur beneath tall beech trees, or oak, spruce, maple or ash, and in North America they are completely dwarfed by majestic Sitka spruce, Douglas fir or Thuja (Western red cedar). Yet this tree, probably more than any other, has the most intriguing stories to tell. Its botany and ecology are full of surprises and unusual solutions for common plant problems (of survival and reproduction), and its cultural history is deep and old and tells us things about ourselves that we will not find anywhere else. Indeed, the multifaceted impact of yew on human life and development omits hardly any of the eternal themes of man: living and dying, health and healing, war and greed, art, science, literature, philosophy and religion.

What the living tree itself did not inspire has been supplied and nourished by its timber or its poison – for in the northern temperate zone yew, box and holly are the only trees that are toxic in all their parts. Only the red flesh that surrounds the yew seed is non-toxic. From this seed grows an evergreen, non-resinous tree. Herein lies the first riddle: the fact that the yew is an evergreen and a conifer without resin and resin ducts. There is a second major conundrum: conifer means 'cone bearing', so where are the cones? Moreover, what are juicy, even sweet fruits doing on a tree with needles for leaves? Is it also not a fact that young tree seedlings in a forest all compete for light and join in a race towards the top of the canopy, in the process becoming rather spindly, long and thin? Yet this is not the case with yew, which grows extremely slowly, both in height and even more so in girth. It does not matter much if it lags behind and in the shade of the others; slowness is part of its ecological strategy, and it has other strengths that offer smarter ways of survival than merely competing for resources.

One such strength is an extraordinary genetic diversity within the species, and a uniquely wide spectrum of morphological plasticity – the variety of form and structure, both visible (trunk, branches, bark, leaves and so on) and invisible (for example photosynthetic organs, leaf stomata and cambium). An encyclopaedia-like short description in the style of a 'technical specification sheet' could never do this tree justice. To state 'leaves: 2–3 cm long', for example, is simply inaccurate when there are also distinctly small-needled yews with no needle longer than 2 cm, and large-needled yews with no needle shorter than 3 cm. The bark may be 'thin, scaly and brown' – if you want to call maroon, bright scarlet, crimson, purple and all possible shades between greys and reds simply 'brown' – but it does not always come off in 'small flakes'. The flakes can be tiny or quite big, and on some trees there are no flakes at all, but rather vertical strips of various lengths that curl off from one end. The trunk can be single-stemmed or multi-stemmed, and the branches can separate at any height, including close to the ground or even at ground level, or for that matter just *below* the ground. The extensive root system feeds them all alike, and being in a way the 'brains' of the tree, it does not care about such irrelevant distinctions.

The overall habit of yew can be described as bearing a rather broad canopy and being of low to medium height that rarely exceeds 15 m

Creeper, Gait Barrows, Cumbria.

(50 ft). This is the small tree found in the understorey in European
beech forests. In Reenadinna, a pure yew rainforest in the Killarney
National Park, Ireland, for example, the old trees are perfectly happy
to keep their heights at 6–14 m (20–46 ft).[1] Yew can, however, also
grow as a bush, or even as a creeper, as can be seen at Gait Barrows
in Cumbria, or on the Irish Atlantic coast. On the other hand, in the
Bavarian Alps, southern France (Ste Baume) and in Italy yews can look
very different, with straight, tall boles that would even make a forester
happy (if they were not standing in national parks). In the Foresta
Umbra on the Gargano peninsula in Italy they reach up to 120 cm
(4 ft) in diameter and heights of 20 m (66 ft) and more. The tallest
yew 'towers' known are about 32 m (105 ft) high. They are located in
the mixed forests of the Caucasus Mountains (Georgia and southern
Russia), a region that has over 130 yew sites, making it one of the
world's biggest yew refuges. However, it is only the monumental yews
of Turkey – with heights reaching 20 m (66 ft) and straight, massive
trunks of almost 8 m (26 ft) in girth – that can remind us of what yew
trees looked like in the ancient world until the timber trade of the

Low growing tree, Grange Fell, Borrowdale, Cumbria.

Roman Empire removed them from the face of the Earth 2,000 years ago.

An entirely different kind of marvel is the high level of vitality of yew, which is unusual for evergreens in the temperate zone. Yew has extraordinary capabilities of vegetative reproduction. It can produce root suckers to enable new trees to emerge from the roots, has the ability to regrow from cuttings, and also produces so-called adventitious growth, when buds appear anywhere on the stem, most often near the base of the trunk where it might be exposed to direct sunlight. Such abilities are highly unusual for 'conifers', yet yew keeps even more trumps up its sleeve. One is branch layering, a process that involves the lower branches growing towards the ground, then taking root. Then there is the growth of vertical branches out of other branches or out of a tumbled trunk, as well as the ability to encase a decaying trunk with secondary wood growth for stability. Most astonishing of all is yew's power to grow an 'interior root' inside a hollowing old trunk, a structure that eventually roots itself in the ground inside the hollow tree, then begins to replace the old decaying trunk until it makes a 'new' tree. This latter function enables a single yew tree to renew itself from the inside out; when this occurs no wood on the tree will be as old as the living being. The discovery that this species has the capability to do this has forced science – or at least botany – to rethink its definition of 'life' for plants. Is a tree that has completely renewed itself still the 'same' tree? Is a living organism truly represented by its body, or by its genetic code or by something else? Is life more than what we can see and touch – and measure?

One way of measuring the vitality of a plant is to monitor its bio-electrical activity. Because the metabolism of living cells is strongly regulated by the electric potential of the minerals they absorb, such as iron, magnesium and potassium, their biochemical metabolism is reflected in their electric potentials. Studies of the electrodynamic force fields of plants commenced at Yale University in 1943.[2] Beginning in June 2004, the Czech scientist Vladimir Rajda conducted a twelve-

Towering monumental yew at Eregli, Turkey.

month study of the geo-phyto electrical currents (GPEC) of yew trees in the Czech Republic.[3] He was in for a few surprises. For one, with GPECs of almost 200 microampere/sq cm (in yews with a trunk diameter of 50 cm/20 in), yew ranks well over other conifers and has an electrical activity twice as strong as that of pine trees. Yew values are comparable to those of broadleaves like beech and ash — which is astonishing because seasonal trees generally have more energy during their shorter activity span than evergreens. Another astonishing fact is that around midwinter, when conifers like spruce 'hibernate', with GPECs close to zero, those of yew never sink below 70 microampere. Yew remains active and 'awake' throughout the winter — it is a true evergreen. Furthermore, yew exhibits a high vitality and significant resistance to environmental (chemical) pollution. With the average health values of the other trees in the country being as low as 68 per cent (the Czech Republic was severely polluted by heavy industries during the communist era), about half of the yew trees in the programme showed vitality levels of 83–7 per cent, while the other half showed '100 per cent vitality'.

All these aspects are hallmarks of a *unique ecological strategy*, one that differs considerably from the strategies of all other forest trees in the temperate zone of the northern hemisphere. To fathom just how different and unique yew is (and the difficulty botanists and taxonomists have in fitting yew into their classification systems), we can take a look at the work of the Swiss botanist Christian Leuthold. He has shown that yew can hardly be systematized at all, either in habit or habitat. Generally, trees have a wide spectrum in how they react to environmental conditions such as soil, temperature changes, drought, neighbouring plants and so on. The ends of this spectrum are marked by the so-called pioneer constitution, trees that venture into open grasslands or wastelands to colonize them for the coming of the forest, and the so-called climax constitution that is typical for trees in the climax stage of a woodland — one that has reached, after various stages of transition, its maximum biomass turnover and a stable equilibrium in the make-up of plant species.

Typical pioneers are birch, Scots pine and juniper, while typical climax trees are beech and oak (although they may occur in earlier transition stages as well). Yew, however, has elements of both ends. For example, it is as resistant to late frosts as pine (unlike beech), but even more shade tolerant than beech (unlike pine). It seems to select the best elements from both worlds to become the versatile survivor that it is. Similarly, in its morphology (shape), it presents elements from across the board: for example, yew leaves are needle shaped, ever-green and long lived, like those of conifers, but their internal structure and energy-efficient composition is more like that of broadleaved trees. All in all, yew inhabits an intermediate position between pioneer and climax species, as well as being a vivid interim between deciduous leaf-bearing trees and evergreen conifers. With its transcendent and primeval characteristics, yew is Europe's oldest tree species, and at the same time, because of its incomparable vitality, the most juvenile. Professor Leuthold dubbed the yew the 'tree archetype of Europe'.[4]

This may provide the impression that yew is a well-researched tree, but this is not the case. For centuries, yew was widely ignored by science in Europe and America because it is not a dominant forest tree. If a tree does not promise large rewards as a producer of timber or food, there usually is not much funding available for research. It was only when a tumour-active substance was discovered in yew bark in 1964 that scientific interest in the tree really began. Most of modern yew knowledge is thus pharmaceutical and biochemical. Almost as a by-product, the tree's general botanical characteristics have been revisited and refined along the way. Many aspects of yew are still, however, only poorly understood.

Equally full of surprises is yew's cultural history. Why did the naturalist and evolutionist Charles Darwin want to be buried beneath the ancient yew of Downe in Kent, a tree he had seen regularly on his daily walks and often paused under? Why were T. S. Eliot, Lewis Carroll, Robert Louis Stevenson and other iconic pioneering writers so fascinated by this tree? Why did Felix Mendelssohn-Bartholdy compose the music for Shakespeare's *Midsummer Night's Dream* beneath two yews? And why was it that yew was present at three key creative impulses of the modern environmental movement? Can a tree be a catalyst for cultural stepping stones?

The cultural impact of yew began well before people with individual names distinguished themselves from the rest of the population. It began in the Old Stone Age, when yew was used to make hunting spears and bows, and continued in the Neolithic period, when it was employed for household items such as bowls, spoons, ladles, mortars and buckets, as well as musical instruments. It was, however, in the use of its wood as foundation piles for lake dwellings where it came into its own. Yew wood is very hard but flexible, extremely durable and highly water resistant. Until relatively recently, it was often used in various countries for fence poles, irrigation pipes, barrel taps and other waterworks. Astonishingly, when 500-year-old pillars underneath some of the palaces in Venice, Italy, were replaced in the nineteenth century, the yew beams were still in a fit state to be refurbished and used elsewhere.[5]

In the Middle Ages the course of history in Europe was changed by the appearance of the deadly yew longbow, but this period also saw the dawn of wonderful yew furniture. An elaborate screen with yew inlay work from outside Europe is over 2,500 years old and stems from the ancient kingdom of Phrygia (in modern Turkey), while yew artefacts from ancient Egyptian graves go back as far as 4,400 years. In Britain, too, the most ancient yew remains from graves are about 4,000 years old and hence predate Celtic culture. The oldest pottery, from Mesopotamia in the Fertile Crescent, shows yew-like branches and is well over 7,500 years old.

The greatest significance of yew in the cultural history of man lies in its spiritual meaning. The vast ages of individual trees and the species' unique abilities of regeneration make the yew the perfect symbol of nature's power of renewal and rebirth. Long before the world's faiths were born as we know them today, the yew was cherished as a 'guardian of the gates' between this world and the next, and employed in a variety of ways in birth and burial customs around

Bowl of a ceremonial pipe in the shape of a raven's head, length *c.* 9.7 cm, *c.* 1850, Tlingit, southeastern Alaska.

the globe. There have been a remarkable number of parallels and similarities in yew traditions over the millennia, in such diverse cultural areas as Ireland, Germany, Scandinavia, Georgia (Caucasus), northern India and Japan. Most of the customs and rituals associated with these traditions have become extinct, but contrary to a widespread belief it was not Christianity that destroyed them – rather, they were overlaid or superseded by other cultural and religious strata over time. What was left of them in Europe was taken by Christianity and incorporated into its own traditions. In nature as in culture, yew is a survivor.

All in all, a comprehensive look at the yew tree cannot be confined to the limits of 'just a tree book'. The study of yew is also a reflection of the plant communities and ecotopes of which yew trees have been a part, as well as a reflection of human cultural history and of our own psyche: the light parts and the dark parts, too.

one

Early Yew

꙳

The species that we know today as the yew tree, *Taxus baccata*, can be traced back to at least the Upper Miocene sub-epoch *c.* 15 million years ago.[1] During the Cenozoic era (66.4 million years ago to the present), the genus *Taxus* has been restricted to the northern hemisphere due to continental drift. Before that, early yews such as *Taxus harisii* and *Marskea jurassica* from the Upper Jurassic epoch co-existed with dinosaurs, including the smaller, winged and feathered dinosaurs that evolved into birds. The yew is 140 million years old and retains most of its early characteristics within the modern genus.[2] Its predecessor, *Palaeotaxus rediviva*, is found in strata dating back 200 million years, and was widely distributed across the global landmass before its separation into continents. The ancestral conifers of these yews, the Taxads, are believed to have evolved from early cone-bearing plants (Voltziaceae family) in the Early Triassic epoch, beginning 248 million years ago. The very earliest conifers date back to the late Carboniferous (360–286 million years ago) and Permian (286–245 million years ago) geological periods.[3]

By comparison, flowering plants (angiosperms) became widespread 100 million years ago, broadleaved trees replaced conifers in areas of milder climates only some 60 million years ago and humans (*Homo*) appeared 2.5 million years ago.

For the younger ecological history of yew we have to switch focus from fossil records to pollen analysis. In general, pollen samples from peat strata or lake deposits are difficult to isolate, and this is particularly true

for yew pollen because the grains are especially tiny and also appear very similar to the pollen of poplar, oak and grasses of the sedge family (*Populus* sp., *Quercus* sp., Cyperaceae), among a number of others. However, pollen records do reveal that yew, to varying degrees, was a constitutive element of the European mixed forest during various interglacial periods. Evidence for this goes back more than 700,000 years to the Cromerian Interglacial period, but the greatest yew density occurred in the warm, oceanic climate of the Hoxnian Interglacial period (400,000–367,000 years ago). In northwest Europe, yew was associated with ash (*Fraxinus*) and alder (*Alnus*) fen woodland with wet soil conditions.[4] During the most recent interglacial period, the Eemian (128,000–115,000 years ago), yew pollen yet again reached significant values, comprising up to 20 per cent of all tree pollen precipitation. For 2,000–3,000 years, *Taxus* was an important species in the mixed pine-oak-hazel-woodland.[5] In some places, such as the

Mondsee Lake in the Northern Alps (Austria) and eastern Upper Bavaria, local values even reached 65 and 80 per cent respectively. In such regions, yew must have constituted about half of the woodland trees.[6] Ultimately, however, a steady decline followed, beginning with climate changes towards the next glacial period, and being amplified by Neolithic people who changed the face of the landscape through the development of settlements, agriculture and pasture.

During the ice ages, yew and its associated plant communities of the temperate zone retreated southwards. The ice ages did not arrive overnight, so trees had many generations to slowly migrate: in America into the southern states, Mexico and even Central America; in Europe to the regions bordering the Mediterranean Sea, and in Asia into the Indian subcontinent. With the end of an ice age approaching, the reverse movement would set in: the trees would migrate from southern China, Laos and Vietnam north and also far west; from India to the southern borderlands of the Himalayas; from Iran to the Caucasus Mountains, and from northern Syria into Turkey. They would similarly again spread over Europe as far north as the British Isles, southern Sweden and the Baltic, and in North America into the coastal regions of both the east and west, as far as British Columbia and Quebec.

After the last ice age retreated and yew regained Central Europe, it reappeared in Germany during the eighth millennium BC. Here it spread continuously and reached a climax in the pine-oak-beech mixed forest of the late warm period from about 3800 BC to almost 3,000 years afterwards.[7] It returned to Britain at the time of the transition from pine (*Pinus*) woodland to mixed deciduous woodland about 7,000 years ago. In the millennium that followed, yew was widespread, and associated with alder, birch, oak and ash. Apart from Scots pine and the rather rare juniper, yew is the only *native* evergreen tree in Britain today.

The continuing rise in temperatures and an acceleration of human influence after the Neolithic period kept changing the landscape and vegetation. Yew had largely disappeared from the eastern Swiss

Mummified seeds, Västergötland, Sweden, Quaternary (approx. 10,000 years old).

Plateau by *c.* 4600 BC,[8] and north of the Alps it declined on peat lands. This was partly compensated for by its spread into drier wood-lands and by it finding new habitats in coppice and other areas of extensive forest management – thus pollen records for Britain, for example, even show a rise for *Taxus* in around 2000 BC. Generally, however, the decline continued. In the very north of Germany and in Denmark, for example, paludification or swamping (the process of bog expansion resulting from rising water tables and peat growth) literally drowned whole yew forests.

Yew decline was not only the result of wetter conditions: it was mainly due to the rise in human populations, and the consequent increases in land use for agriculture and pasture. The Middle Ages in Europe saw fast-growing populations, ever-increasing land use and the need for timber for the wooden architecture of whole cities – including their regular reconstruction after catastrophic fires – as well as for the rising new fuel-consuming industries for metal, salt and glass production. Europe would have become a desert if the climate had not been ideal for fast reforestation, at least with Norway spruce and Scots pine. The foundations for modern forestry were laid in Germany with the pine plantations that began in 1750, as the only possible answer to vast areas of barren wastelands left by non-sustainable land abuse – that is, deforestation. The effects of the early industrial age would have taken an even greater toll on Europe if it had not been for massive wood imports from the colonies in America, Africa and New Zealand.[9]

Taxus baccata did, however, survive in almost all the countries of its natural distribution, despite the small numbers in certain regions – and it never stopped exerting its influence on human culture.

two

Botanical Yew

🜎

L ooking at the botany of the yew reveals that it has many stunning and unique features. It also contradicts a few widespread assumptions: for example, *Taxus baccata* is not just a resident of cool and wet northern countries but can adapt to a whole spectrum of local climates; and it has an arsenal of survival strategies for different ecological challenges.

Climate and Distribution

The yew grows best in climates that provide mild winters and cool summers. A sufficient water supply, usually provided by rainfall, is important to its growth, although high humidity, for example from frequent mists, can counterbalance a lack of precipitation to some extent. Indeed, yew is often found in areas of a region that have the highest rainfall, such as the Reenadinna rainforest in southwest Ireland and the Pacific rainforest of North America. Particularly important is the rainfall in July and August, when the leaf buds for the next year are formed, and in March to May, when the present year's leaf buds swell and open.[1] Yew trees require a minimum average precipitation of 500–1,000 mm annually, and are perfectly fine with rainforest conditions of 1,500–2,000 mm annually.[2] The only condition yew will not tolerate is stagnant water, since swamping and bog-like conditions suffocate yew roots. Other factors restricting yew growth are severe winter cold, late frosts, and cold and drying winds in exposed positions.

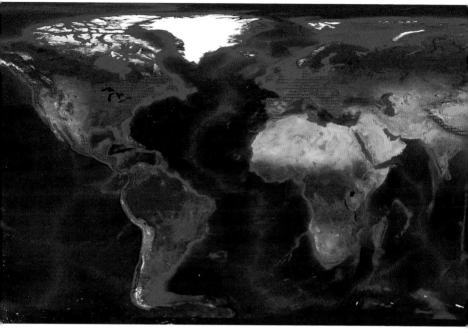

The natural distribution of *Taxus* worldwide.

The water demand makes yew a tree of the temperate zone, where it finds ideal conditions in the mild oceanic climate of the coastal regions. Where it ventures south, into the subtropical zone, it balances the dryer and warmer weather with greater altitudes. Hence yew is found at between o and around 470 m (1,550 ft) above sea level in Britain, but at 1,000–1,400 m (3,280–4,594 ft) in the Alps, up to 2,000 m (6,562 ft) in Greece, up to 3,330 m (10,925 ft) in Guatemala and at 2,800–3,570 m (9,300–11,900 ft) in south-western China (Yunnan).[3]

The temperature range for photosynthesis in yew is extraordinarily large, and encompasses that of all other European tree species. Yew can thus photosynthesize throughout the (mild) winter, which is especially useful for yews standing in the lower tier beneath broad-leaved trees such as ash or beech that are bare in winter. This is quite important because it makes up for yew's rather low photosynthetic effectiveness during the summer half of the year. In winter, yew can

assimilate (photosynthesize) in temperatures down to −8°C (17.6°F). Its summer temperature maximum for photosynthetic activity is 38–41°C (100.4–105.8°F).[4] Yew is intolerant, however, of severe and prolonged frost and icy winds. Frost tolerance changes with the seasons, its maximum occurring in winter (January), and the least tolerance occurring in early spring, when the opening buds begin to expose vulnerable tissues. Frost tolerance also varies with geography: in Britain, winter frost damage can start at −13.4°C (7.8°F), and by March tolerance shrinks to −9.6°C (14.7°F) in the hardiest area (southern England) and even to −1.9°C (28.5°F) in the most susceptible area (northeast England).[5] In Japan, yew bears severe frost down to −40°C (−40°F) before needle damage occurs.[6]

Heat resistance does not vary significantly in the course of the year. Half an hour of 48–50°C (118–122°F) will damage needles, while about 44°C (111°F) is a limit for the sensitive buds and young needles in spring.[7] Yews in comparatively dry, hot climates have a higher heat tolerance than those in cool northern countries, which is no surprise because adaptation has taken place. The thin bark of yew does not protect it from fire, as does the thick cork padding of, for example, redwood trees (*Sequoia*). Luckily, the absence of resin renders yew's combustibility much lower than that of other conifers.[8] Additionally, yews are protected from fires because most 'forest' fires in the subtropics are actually savannah fires, and yews tend to grow in mixed forests at higher elevations. Many fires (even in pine plantations) actually stop at the edges of old forests, such as those of live oak (*Quercus rotundifolia*) in Spain.[9]

The ecological factors that set the boundaries for yew distribution are low temperatures in the north, severe continental climate with cold winters and hot, dry summers (east of Poland, central North America, and inland in northeast China and eastern Siberia), and drought and high temperature in the south (Mexico, northwest Africa,

overleaf: Hollow old yew at Newlands Corner, Surrey, where over 130 yew trees have been recorded.

Iran and Anatolia). Near these extremes, yew becomes restricted to moist niches such as river valleys, or to cool and moist higher elevations. Yew extends northwards to southern Norway and southwards to Algeria (Atlas Mountains), in Central America down to Mexico and Guatemala (high-altitude rainforests), and in Asia as far south as Vietnam, the Philippines and Indonesia (Sumatra and Sulawesi), the latter being the only country where yew grows south of the equator.

Taxonomy

The yew, botanical name *Taxus baccata* L., belongs to the gymnosperms – a classification term for plants with seeds that do not develop in an ovary ('naked seeds'). This group also includes the subtropical and tropical cycads, the ginkgo tree and, of course, the conifers such as pines, redwoods, firs, spruces and cypresses. In contrast to the reproductive structures of the gymnosperms, the seeds of angiosperms (commonly known as 'flowering plants') develop in an ovary. The broadleaved trees belong to this group.

Throughout the history of plant classification, the position of yew has been controversial. It has been placed among the conifers, in the order Coniferales. However, conifer means 'cone bearing', and the fleshy cup that surrounds the yew seed is anything but a cone. Moreover, cones usually carry one or more seeds inside each protecting scale, but yew bears the characteristic of an entirely single ovule. Hence some authorities, for example Stewart in 1983,[10] have separated yews from the Coniferales into a distinct order of their own: Taxales ('yew-like'). This makes a lot of sense, but has created other conundrums. However, a little tweak in the actual definition of conifer (in 2002) helped to keep yew commonly classified as a conifer.[11] Two things are for sure: yew is yew, and the controversy will remain.

The discourse whether yew occurs as one or many species has been even fiercer than the one about the positioning of the yew family in the wider system. When Carl Linnaeus introduced the binomial nomenclature in the first edition of his book, *Systema Naturae*, in 1753, he listed yew as *one* species: the European yew, *Taxus baccata* L. The Latin name of the genus *Taxus* is identical to the tree's ancient Roman name. The species name *baccata* means 'berry-bearing', which is incorrect when applied to the fleshy cup around the yew seed, since it is not a berry but an aril. Linnaeus knew the yew as occurring in Europe, and also in Canada. During the twentieth century, some botanists divided the genus *Taxus* into eight species (between seven and eleven in different systems), which correspond to the geographical distribution areas: European (or English) yew, Pacific yew, Canadian yew, Japanese yew, Himalayan yew and so on.[12] Other botanists kept the view that it was one species only. In 1903, Robert Pilger put forward a strong case for a single species named *Taxus baccata* and classified all geographical yews as subspecies of it. This view was confirmed in 2012 as results from genetic research finally began to emerge. Genetic studies reveal a 'large uniformity in the different taxa', says Professor B. Schirone, project leader of the Mediterranean Forest DNA Bank. He states that 'at the genotypic level there is no chance to discriminate between *T. baccata* and *T. wallichiana* [the European and the Himalayan yew], which do not appear as clearly distinct species', but

Yew rainforest at Killarney, Ireland.

rather as mere geographic differentiations of the same species 'whose range split in remote times'.[13] After all, even in botanical terms, the various (sub)species are incredibly similar to each other. There is also an exceptionally wide spectrum of morphological plasticity within *Taxus baccata* in Europe alone. Of course, geography leaves its marks: populations existing in different climate conditions are bound to develop some physical alterations to buffer their environmental conditions. However, this does not necessarily make them different species — in the same way as a brown-eyed Indian and a blue-eyed Scandinavian are both *Homo sapiens sapiens*. The argument that yew is a single species is supported by the fact that when different yew 'species' grow near each other, hybrids frequently occur. Moreover, 70 garden cultivars — according to some sources even over 100 — have been bred from *Taxus baccata*. This provides further proof of the immense potential and adaptability of yew's genetics.

The Root System

The root system of yew is nothing like the shallow root plates of broadleaves such as beech or conifers like spruce. It is dense, extensive and deep. Its effective penetration of the soil facilitates an efficient supply of water and minerals to the tree. It also lends excellent mechanical support in even the most challenging of terrains, such as rock pavements and vertical cliffs. Even as a seedling, *Taxus* invests primarily in its root system.[14] At all growth stages, and during good times as well as in periods of limited growth, the strengthening of the root system has priority over height and girth increase — even in dense forest, the option of competing with other trees for light does not alter this strategy. This is an integral part of the ecological strategy of yew. Together with narrow xylem tubes (a general characteristic in *Taxus*), a well-developed root system is a safety measure employed by yew that considerably limits the dangers of droughts. Bio-electric studies confirm that yew employs the root system with the highest vitality among trees.[15] The roots maintain activity throughout the

Remarkable yew roots at Merdon Castle, Hampshire.

winter months. They store energy in the form of carbohydrates not only for the opening of buds in spring, like other trees, but also for 'bad times', making the tree unusually tolerant of periods of water or light deficiency. An intense root system that is perfectly adapted to its habitat is also the firm base for the unique regenerative abilities of yew.[16]

Yew roots are additionally capable of penetrating compressed soils and finding their way through bare rock. Furthermore, there is no competition underground: the roots of other trees seem to have no bearing on the density of yew roots.[17]

Alas, there is one thing that even yew roots cannot do: that is live without a fungus. All trees, like higher plants in general, live in symbiosis (a mutually beneficial relationship) with certain types of fungus whose network of tubular filaments, or hyphae, is a significant extension to their root system. Additionally, the fungus is able to transform inorganic chemical substances from the soil into organic plant nutrients (minerals), which the plant can absorb. In return, the plant supplies the fungus with carbohydrates and amino acids, nutrients the fungus cannot produce because it cannot perform photosynthesis. This symbiosis of tree and fungus is called mycorrhiza. Of the three general types of mycorrhiza, the only one occurring in *Taxus* is endomycorrhiza, in which the hyphae grow intracellularly – that is, the fungal filaments do not just penetrate the tree root in between its cells, but in yew roots also grow *into* the cells. As for the identification of the fungi that grow with yew, research in this field is young but studies in Iran have revealed seven species from the genera *Glomus*, *Acaulospora* and *Gigaspora*.[18]

Yew is most often found on soils based on limestone or chalk. These soils are favoured when yew is growing near the boundaries of its climatic distribution, where the other conditions are more strenuous. However, when yew is located within a region with optimum conditions, it can grow on a very wide variety of soils. Indeed, it can be almost any soil, typically a deep, well-drained humus and base-rich soil of variable pH, although yew also thrives on shallow, dry rendzinas on limestone, on thin, warm chalk soils and even on calcareous peat in fens. Yew can additionally be found on sandy soils or loamy sand if there is enough moisture, and on siliceous soils derived from igneous and sedimentary rocks. In the Mediterranean, the ancient yews of Sardinia thrive on schist, granite, chalk and basalt.[19] The only two ground conditions that *Taxus* avoids are those with poor drainage and high acidity.

Another interesting observation is that yews do not just adapt to their immediate locality, but can also change some of the attributes of the soils in which they grow. In comparison to humic acids under oak trees, for example, those under yew trees become more oxidized and have a lower mineral content, but they are significantly richer in carbon, nitrogen and calcium, which is thought to be caused by the absence of large earthworms under yew.[20]

One of the most difficult grounds to cling to: steep and loose talus slope, at Low Scawdel, Borrowdale, Cumbria. Because of poor nutrition and high winds, this tree is likely to be much older than its girth would suggest.

New leaves in the sunlight.

The Foliage

The other main supply system of trees, apart from the roots, is located in the leaves (including 'needles', because in botany a needle is just one possible shape that a leaf can adopt). The foremost function of the leaves of higher plants is photosynthesis. Despite its relatively short name, photosynthesis is a highly complex chain of events that, at its bottom line, uses solar energy to convert water and carbon dioxide into a number of energy-rich organic compounds (carbohydrates), which the tree can use to produce wood, feed all types of its tissue or store as cell food for the future.

Unlike water, sunlight is generally readily available in all climates. However, the light quantities vary with the length of daytime during the seasons and with the individual position of a plant, which can involve shading by objects such as rocks, hill slopes, houses or other trees. Like any other plant, yew needs a sufficient amount of light, but in this respect too it has an unusually wide spectrum of tolerance. On the one hand, its ability to bear direct sun exposure is demonstrated by specimens growing on exposed rocks and cliff faces. On the other hand, and more famously, yew has a remarkable shade tolerance – which does not mean, as many people think, that it *prefers* shadow. Indeed, *Taxus* is the most shade-tolerant tree in Europe. If the (low) shade tolerance of birch is given at the virtual value of 1, and spruce at 2 (meaning that spruce can still assimilate at only half the light value at which birch has to stop), the 'classical' shade tree of Western Europe, fir, has a shade tolerance of 2.2. This sets the range within which the values for all other trees can be found. Yew is, however, far out, with a shade tolerance of 5.8. This is more in league with the forest herbs that cover the shady ground than with shrubs and trees.[21] Ideal for yew, however, is the half shade of deciduous trees, with ash and alder being particularly favourable because in their company it usually also finds a good water supply.

The needle-shaped leaves of yew vary in length. They are usually 16–25 mm (⅝–1 in) long, but in some trees can be as short as 10 mm (½ in) or as long as 45 mm (2 in). Their usual width is 2–3 mm (less than ¼ in). Their colour is dark glossy green above and clearly paler on the underside. They are soft, have parallel sides and short stalks, and end in a short, non-stinging tip. On the twigs they are neatly parted into two ranks, but on shoots they are spirally attached. Yew leaves live for four to eight years, but their photosynthetic ability declines with age, to only 50 per cent in seven-year-old needles compared with young ones.[22]

The needles' anatomy does not possess the mechanical support tissue (sclerenchyma) that is typical of conifers,[23] so the leaves of yew are unusually soft for an evergreen. This makes them a favourite of browsing animals like deer and rabbits, despite the toxins they contain. (The ancient Greeks called the yew *elate*, or 'soft fir'.) The leaf

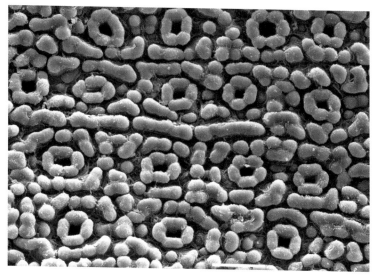

The stomata (electron microscope image).

surface consists of an outer skin, the epidermis, which is covered with a protective wax layer, the cuticle (cuticula). On the lower surface of the leaf, the cuticle forms irregular thickenings, particularly near the stomata – minute pores in the leaf of a higher plant. They serve the gas exchange (carbon dioxide, CO_2, and oxygen, O_2) and the almost constant release of excess water. The stomata of *Taxus* are visible in two bands on the underside of a leaf, but they are not arranged in actual lines within these bands, as stomata in some other species are. Yew leaves have 59 to 119 stomata per square millimetre (for comparison, Scots pine leaves have about 100). Yew stomata are sunk into the epidermis, which minimizes air movement and evaporation, but cuticular waxes, which assist the regulation of water transpiration in other conifers, are absent in yew. Instead, its stomata are surrounded by elevated subsidiary cells. Their swelling and shrinking controls the opening of the stomata and thereby the gas exchange and – important in times of drought – the water release. Yew stomata are capable of incredibly fast responses to changing weather conditions.[24]

Underneath the epidermis lies a thin stratum of one to three cell layers called the palisade parenchyma – parenchyma is the name for plant tissue made up of undifferentiated and usually unspecialized cells. The majority of the photosynthetically active chlorophyll grains are embedded here. Moving inwards, the next layer of tissue is the spongy parenchyma, which makes up the bulk of the leaf matter. The relationship between the two parenchyma types depends on the light conditions during the growth of a leaf. Indeed, in this respect yew has different types of leaf: distinct light leaves with a maximum of palisade parenchyma containing chlorophyll grains, and distinct shadow leaves that are specialized in making the most of the little light they get. Distinct shadow leaves only occur well below 1 per cent light intensity. Another difference between the leaf types is that the cuticula of light leaves is stronger than that in shadow leaves and hence gives additional water-loss protection. This means that if shadow branches are suddenly exposed to sunlight the tree is in danger of too much water loss.[25] Single leaves cannot be 'switched' once they are fully developed. It can be a major challenge to a yew if the whole tree or a large part of it is suddenly exposed to direct sunlight. This can be caused by the disappearance of a long-term shading object, for example when a neighbouring tree is felled by a storm, by age or by human interference. Yew leaves are only replaced every four to eight years and that

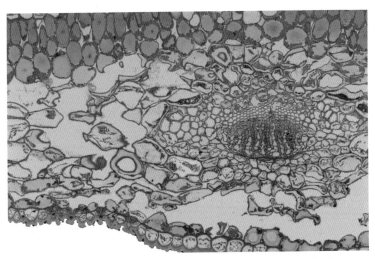

Cross-cut of leaf (Azorean lineage), electron microscope image (dyed).

is how long the adaptation to the new light situation would take. During this period, particularly in the beginning, the yew's vital balance would be impaired, and in the worst case the tree could even die. This is an essential consideration for gardeners, park rangers and church wardens.

Yew seedlings are able to develop with extraordinarily low light values (only 1 per cent or less of the light exposure in the open), and more light does not make them grow faster. Sexually mature trees are capable of producing sufficient numbers of seeds even at well below 5 per cent relative light intensity. However, female yews do produce more flowers under higher light exposure.[26] There is another surprise at the other end of the scale: the net performance of photosynthesis in *Taxus* is extraordinarily low even under optimum conditions. Yews are not capable of using a higher light exposure effectively. This means that in periods of great summer heat, a yew loses a lot of energy because of increased respiration and its inability to balance this with a more effective photosynthesis. However, as mentioned above, yew makes up for it by photosynthesizing through the winter, when there is more moisture in the soil and more light because the deciduous trees of the upper tier are bare of leaves, so it creates stores of excess energy

A fallen twig frozen in water.

that last well into the warmer half of the year.[27] Once again, these are signs of its ecological strategy, 'according to which the safeguarding of a low but constant growth independent from exterior influences contributes to the ability of survival', in the words of yew expert Ulrich Pietzarka of the Saxonian State Arboretum, Tharandt, Germany.[28]

Carbohydrate reserves (sugars such as fructose, glucose and sucrose) can be found in yew all year round. The sucrose content is higher than that in other conifers investigated, namely Scots pine, larch and hemlock. A major part of the sugar reserves is stored in the form of hemicellulose in the needles of the previous year and released in spring for the development of new needles and shoots. Over half of yew's nitrogen reserves exists in the form of the amino-acid argenine, similar to apple and pear trees.[29]

Sexual Reproduction

Generally *Taxus* is a dioecious tree (from the ancient Greek word for 'two households'), as male and female reproductive organs are borne on different trees. Bisexual trees exist but are rare; the frequency usually reported is 1–2 per cent of trees.[30] Bisexual trees usually bear only single branches of one of the genders. A change in the sex of an individual tree is also possible,[31] particularly in extremely isolated specimens, but can also occur in locations where yews are abundant, much to the puzzlement of foresters.[32] Actually, the real numbers of bisexual yews may be significantly higher than anyone knows. This is because the gender of a yew tree is usually 'identified' at first glance – when a few scarlet fruits are spotted a tree is documented as 'female', and on the sight of some male flowers or their buds it is recorded as 'male'.

For plants (as well as animals), sexual reproduction is essential because it creates new individuals with a *unique* genetic make-up, an important ecological strategy especially for small isolated populations of species that run a high risk of losing part of their genetic information. Often enough, the consequence of a low population

Pollen release in early spring.

Yew colonizing a limestone hillside in subtropical Sardinia.

size in the long run is a decrease in the range of genotypes (that is, of the special constellations of inherited characteristics). However, it is this very variety of genotypes that is the guarantor of long-term survival. It gives a species more facilities for dealing with environmental challenges. Epidemics, for example, often strike certain genotypes, while others are more tolerant. Interestingly, genetic research has shown that yew populations, for all their scarcity and small sizes, are remarkably diverse in comparison to other conifers. Yews are able to pass on to their offspring a high amount of new information brought in by pollen from outside the stand. This biological success story is made possible by a number of adaptations.

First of all, yew pollen grains are incredibly numerous and also very light – in still air they sink at a speed of only about 2 cm (½ in) per second, which is even slower than the pollen-grain speed of the pioneer tree, birch, and twenty times slower than that of fir. Hence they can travel far indeed. To avoid all females in one cluster becoming fertilized by one 'alpha male' (the one that sheds its pollen first or just stands closest to them), individual *Taxus* trees (or genotypes) flower at slightly different times. Even in a close yew community, therefore, the females are pollinated at different times by pollen clouds from different male trees.[33] Apart from these two general measures, *Taxus* has another means of ensuring cross-pollination at its disposal: the above-mentioned sex change of single twigs, branches or entire trees.

Note that this last subject can reveal how much morals and paradigms may impair our judgement of facts. By simply hearing that yew occurs 'generally' as a tree with either male or female flowers, and 'rarely' as bisexual or with a documented change of sex, we may more or less subconsciously assume that there are four types of yew tree: two 'normal' ones (male and female), and two 'strange' ones (bisexual and sex changed) that are exceptions to the rule. This perception may be coloured even further by our individual projections of 'similar phenomena' in human society. Forget all this – this is the forest, thirteen million years before humanoids were even on the horizon.

The University of Tuscia (Viterbo, Italy) has recently conducted an extensive study of the sexual behaviour of *Taxus*. The preliminary results suggest some daring new insights. Changing gender is an adaptation of the species' gene pool to climatic variation and changeability, to enable the species to autoregulate the sex ratio in a population to maximize reproduction efforts. Sex reversal is a reproductive strategy, genetically fixed at species level but expressed only by small (and usually struggling) populations, and foremost in populations at the boundaries of *Taxus* distribution. At the individual level, too, changing gender is a reproductive strategy that is performed when environmental conditions require change. Hence, monoecism of a single tree is not a permanent status but a momentary 'picture' that we take. Monoecism of a single tree may be the basic condition for *Taxus*, but it is only revealed in a short time frame and affected by environmental conditions.[34]

Some of these statements need further research and verification, but to us normal mortals the message is already emerging: there are really no 'male' and 'female' yews. There is only *one* type of yew tree – which can assume all these forms. Any individual tree might display the other gender next year. It may be highly unlikely that it will, and it may not change for 500 or 1,000 years (albeit older trees change less readily than young ones). The potential is, however, present in each individual.

Possessing all the above characteristics in terms of population genetics, yew is perfectly adapted to living in small, isolated stands.

In single yew trees and open stands, sexual maturity (or shall we say decision making?) usually starts at 30–35 years of age. In dense woods it can begin as late as 70–120 years of age.[35] Under the dense shade of a beech canopy a yew tree may not flower at all, but wait for a couple of hundred years until the beech trees have died. The small green flower buds are formed in the leaf axils during the second half of summer. They open in the following spring – in mild climates in February or March, and as late as April to May only in locations where winter snows or coldness endure. The early release of the pollen facilitates optimum distribution because during this time the deciduous trees have no leaves to obstruct pollen flight.

Yew flowers are tiny. The male flowers are 2–3 mm ($^1/_{16}$–$^2/_{16}$ in) in diameter, the female flowers about a third smaller. However, they are rather abundant, at least on trees in the open, and the myriads of male flowers often tinge the overall green impression of a tree towards a beige, sand-coloured or yellowish look. The male flowers consist of six to fourteen short-stalked stamens (microsporophylls), each with four to nine pollen sacs (microsporangia). Once warm weather stimulates them to open, the slightest air movement stirs the release of the pollen grains. A slightly stronger movement of the branches even creates a visible golden-yellow cloud. The pollen grains are wind borne,

Male flower buds in late winter.

but this does not stop honeybees, or many different species of small fly, beetle and other insect, from occasionally visiting the flowers. Wind pollination naturally implies a high loss of pollen, compared with the precise, 'spot-on' pollination by insects that dedicatedly fly from flower to flower. *Taxus* counterbalances this by producing extraordinarily large amounts of pollen; the pollen count per flower is higher than in any other conifer and suffices to secure a 100 per cent pollination of the female flowers.[36]

The female flowers appear solitary or paired. They consist of several overlapping scales, of which the uppermost is fertile and usually bears a single ovule, or two on rare occasions.[37] At the tip of the flower the outer layer (integument) forms a tiny canal, which is sealed at the outer end with a drop of sticky, sugary liquid. The function of this so-called micropylar drop (or pollination drop) is to catch pollen grains. Just over 1,000 pollen grains can be caught by its surface – 260 times the amount that is necessary to secure fertilization.[38] This again shows that the yew's ecological strategy prioritizes safety.

Saturated with a sufficient number of pollen grains, the pollination drop and the pollen therein are reabsorbed by the nucellus and

Single male flower, before and after spilling its pollen.

sink down into the pollen chamber, where the pollen begins to germinate. While the pollen grains of many tree species are actually round or oval, yew pollen is dehydrated so that it looks rather shrivelled, but this characteristic gives it even less weight for a successful long-haul flight. During germination inside the female flower, the pollen grain swells to a full spherical shape, then bursts open. A pollen tube grows out of it and towards the egg cell, which it reaches after ten days. The ensuing biological process finally sees the male and female gametes (reproductive cells) wrap themselves in a mutual

Female flower with micropylar drop.

coat of cytoplasm, then merge. The life of the embryo begins. The overall time from pollination to fertilization is usually six to eight weeks (in rare cases up to three months).[39]

From the moment of fertilization the embryo takes about three months to develop – hence the visible fruit is ready in late summer. With a length of 1.2–1.5 mm ($^1/_{16}$ in), the embryo is rather small compared with the entire seed, which measures about 5 mm ($^1/_4$ in) in diameter. The embryo occupies the upper part of the seed (the end opposite the stalk). The whitish tissue surrounding and nourishing the embryo is the endosperm, which is rich in reserve substances, mainly proteins and fats. The whole seed in its woody shell is highly toxic to humans and most other mammals. The surrounding cup of red pulp is not and is the only non-toxic part of the tree (but beware, the *green* pulp is toxic too).

Despite the tree's botanical name (*baccata* = berry bearing), yew produces neither a fruit (gymnosperms do not have 'fruits') nor a berry. Fruits develop from the ovaries of angiosperms, and so do berries. Arils are fruit-like structures that develop from a different part of the reproductive structure – from the area where the seed

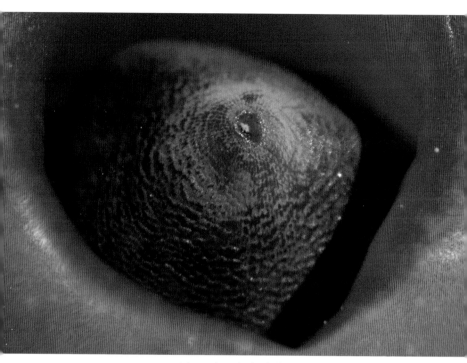

The seed inside the fleshy red aril.

is attached to the plant. In colloquial language, 'fruits' are sweet and edible structures that surround plant seeds, and 'berry' is a term for any small edible fruit – in this sense, the yew aril may be called a fruit.

The aril of yew is bright scarlet red (in some garden varieties orange or golden), and contains a juicy, sweet-tasting and somewhat slimy pulp that is highly nutritious. Measurements of the moisture content of yew arils vary from about 31 per cent (in Poland) to more than 60 per cent (Spain).[40] The dry pulp consists of 94 per cent carbohydrates, 2.6 per cent fibre, 2.3 per cent protein, 1.4 per cent ash (that is, minerals) and 0.2 per cent lipids. The mineral content is, in g/100g: calcium 0.2, magnesium 0.1, phosphorus 0.4, potassium 6.0, sodium 0.2, and in mg/100g: iron 25, manganese 1, zinc 5, copper 1.[41] The main function of the aril is to attract birds, which are the main agent of seed distribution. Some mammals, for example foxes and badgers, also eat yew arils. The seeds pass through the digestive tracts of birds and mammals, and

are dispersed on the forest floor with a good portion of dung. This
sets the stage for the next chapter in the natural regeneration of a
tree species: germination and survival as a seedling. The seeds of most
conifers require a winter period of cold, moist stratification before
they will germinate. The absorption of water, the passage of time,
the rhythms of temperature changes, oxygen availability and light
exposure all take part in initiating the process. For the yew, another
component is suspected, namely the passage of the arils through the
digestive tracts of birds. For one, this process separates the seeds from
the arils, which must be removed for successful germination, otherwise
viability can go down to about 2 per cent.[42] It has also been assumed
that components in a bird's colon may give additional chemical stimulation to the seed coat.[43] However, *Taxus* seed still rarely germinates
in the first year; this process usually takes place in the second or even
third year.

The long dormancy of the seed represents yet another expression
of the yew's ecological strategy of slowness and safety: it increases
the chances of germination in favourable weather conditions, and
also creates an assured seed bank in the ground that is accessible in
the case of a poor flowering year. The price to pay is a prolonged risk
of fungal infection or rodent predation. This is not as serious as it may
sound because the viability of yew seeds can be extraordinarily high,
approaching 100 per cent, although germination rates of 50–70 per
cent are more usual – and still high. The seed can remain fertile for
up to four years.[44]

Then comes the difficult bit. More than half of yew seedlings do
not make it to the sapling phase. The annual mortality rate is about 10
per cent on average. In most plant species, the vast majority of seeds
and seedlings never succeed, but for yew there is higher browsing
pressure because deer, hares and rabbits know that yew foliage is soft
to the tongue and full of carbohydrates and amino acids. Rodents like
mice do further damage to seeds and young roots. Yew's slow growth

overleaf: The contorted fragments of the trunk of the ancient yew at Llanerfyl, Powys.
In 1998 the total girth measured 1067 cm.

does not ease the problem. After about two years a seedling reaches sapling stage with the beginning of side shoot development, but it is still only 10 cm (4 in) high and prone to be bitten back to ground level. If left alone, the sapling reaches the juvenile phase at between ten and sixty years, but usually after about twenty. The young tree is now 50 cm–2 m (20 in–6½ ft) high and has doubled its annual height increase to 4–8 cm (1½–3 in). The rate of annual height gain keeps increasing until the tree has reached about 4 m (13 ft 4 in), but it is still clearly below that of all other European trees (even including the other species of the lower tier, such as box and holly) and can only be compared with that of juniper (*Juniperus communis*). Only above 1.35 m (4 ft 6 in) does foliage begin to be safe from deer browsing. Damage to the central shoot (apical shoot) is also the reason why some yew trees become multi-stemmed from an early age. Another important cause of this is the bud gall mite *Cecidophyes psilaspis*, which overwinters in the bud and can contribute significantly to the damage of apical shoots if it returns annually. Yew is capable of balancing the loss of its apex by raising one or more of the upper side shoots to take its place. A third reason for multi-stemmed shapes lies in *Taxus* itself: 10–35 per cent of young yews naturally have competing apical shoots (on average three to six).[45]

The whole process of reproduction of a local tree population is called 'natural rejuvenation' or 'regeneration', or 'recruitment' in forestry terms. In all temperate countries of Europe and Asia, sufficient yew rejuvenation is jeopardized by deer pressure. Deer fences or wire tubes for single trees are the only solution, at least for limited areas, but they are expensive. The reasons for the extensive deer populations are the absence of their natural enemies (wolves, lynx, foxes and bears) and the high political influence of hunters. 'A bad hunter', says a joke among the desperate foresters, 'needs many deer to hit *one*'.

The Wooden Structure

A protective layer of bark covers the structural wooden parts of a tree and, more importantly, its living tissues. The bark of the yew is usually reddish-brown, thin and odourless, and has a slightly bitter and astringent taste. Old layers of bark are irregularly shed in thin, flat scales (in some trees in strips) along the outside. On the inside, bark regrows from the bark cambium.

The essential living tissue of a tree, the cambium, is a thin layer located just beneath the bark and bark cambium. Along its outer circumference it produces phloem cells, and on the inside it produces xylem cells. Phloem and xylem constitute two independent transport systems that connect every rootlet of a tree with every single leaf. The xylem cells form continuous channels that distribute the water absorbed by the roots, and the minerals contained therein, to all parts of the tree. The 'sieve cells' or 'sieve tubes' of the phloem form continuous channels that transport the nutritious sap of assimilates created by the leaves to the growing seeds and fruits, or downwards to facilitate wood growth in the branches and trunk, or further down to the roots where it can be stored and redistributed in later periods. To avoid the danger that injuries (mechanical ones from falling rocks or other trees, or unintentional ones from drilling woodpeckers, for example) would cause, leading to excessive loss of this precious liquid, higher plants (including trees) have developed so-called sieve plates that occur at frequent intervals in all phloem channels. They can interrupt the sap stream and shut it down like an emergency valve.

While phloem cells stay alive and live for quite some time, xylem cells follow a different plan. When they have reached their destined shape and size, they die. The inner core and everything inside the cell wall gets cleaned out, leaving only a hollow but strong tube of cellulose, which is additionally strengthened by the incorporation of substances such as lignin. After functioning as part of the water-transport system in the sapwood for a year or longer, old xylem cells increasingly become blocked and finally retire. Chemical changes convert them to heartwood, whose primary function is the mechanical support of the trunk and crown. Because xylem cells produced in spring (early wood) are larger and have thinner walls than those produced towards the end of the growth season (late wood), annual

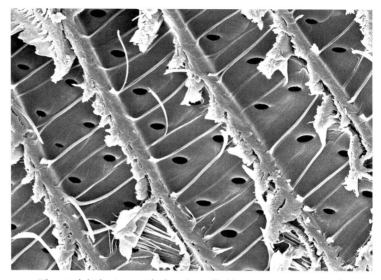

The spiral thickenings inside the xylem cells (electron microscope image).

rings of trees can be seen with the bare eye in cross-cuts of trunks or branches. In yew, the reddish heartwood is distinct from the pale sapwood, which is usually about ten to twenty annual rings thick.[46]

Because yew is very slow growing its annual rings are rather narrow, roughly about half the width of the other tree species of the temperate mixed forests. Of course, local conditions always leave their mark: for example, wood from low altitudes is likely to have broader rings than wood from mountainous areas, and long winters or dry summers slow down wood growth as well. Overall, yew's extremely slow growth makes its wood hard, heavy and durable. Its high density is reflected in its weight, 640–800 kg/m³, which is well above the values of other evergreens (redwood 420, pine 510), and is more comparable with those of broadleaves such as beech and oak (720).[47]

Yew wood is not only hard, but also highly flexible. It is this combination that has made it so desirable to man ever since the first hunting spear, found at Clacton-on-Sea, Essex, was produced from it two ice ages ago (in the Hoxnian interglacial, 200,000–300,000 years BC).[48] This high flexibility is made possible by an important

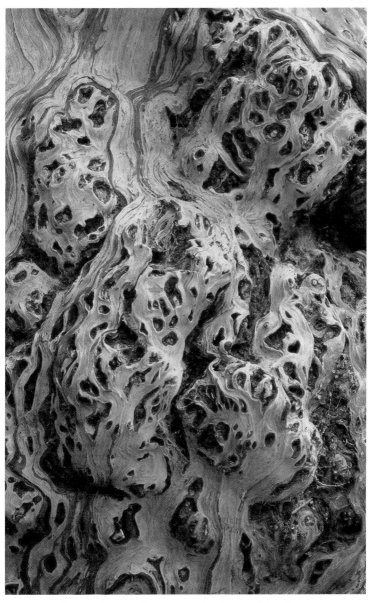

The secondary growth in yew wood is often gnarled and curvy.

The markedly fluted trunk of the ancient yew at West Tisted, Hampshire.

anatomical feature that yew shares with the other trees of the order Taxales: the spiral thickenings of the tracheids (or xylem channel cells). In yew they are particularly strongly developed. Additionally, with a mean diameter of 18.4μm (micrometres), yew tracheids are the narrowest among all European tree species,[49] and add strength to the wood.

In common with other trees, the sapwood and heartwood of yew have rays to facilitate radial (horizontal) water transport. On average they are one to fifteen cells high.[50]

The above points may explain the main characteristics of wood from straight trees in timber-production forests. In yew, however, we have to look at a number of additional types of structure. The first

Hollow grooves beneath branches are a sign of low nutrition.

one is *secondary wood*: since the hollowing of the trunks of ageing yew trees is a general characteristic in yew, the load-bearing stresses on a supporting trunk repeatedly need readdressing. As a result, new growth has to be laid down in various areas around the increasingly thin-walled trunk. This regenerative or secondary growth is usually even less straight grained than the original wood; it is of a rather curvy, winding and flowing nature. Next, yew has a tendency to create *fluted trunks*, much more pronounced than in hornbeam (*Carpinus betulus*), for example. One theory to explain this is that parts of the root might die off and the corresponding vertical sections of the trunk become undernourished and thereby slimmer than the neighbouring strips of cambium. However, given the incredible strength of the *Taxus* root system there is no reason to suspect that such partial root 'failure' should occur at all, let alone at such frequent, almost ornamental intervals. In German forestry and arboriculture, the phenomenon of fluted trunks has long been shown to be the result of (usually lower) branches growing in extreme shade. With a yew canopy usually being rather dense, this applies to many yew branches. The low photosynthetic rate of *Taxus* only creates enough nutrients to keep a branch alive and slowly growing, but leaves no big surplus to facilitate wood growth below the branch. A hollow groove therefore begins in the 'armpit', as it were, of the branch and continues all the way down.[51]

A third irregularity in yew wood is the 'peppered' effect that makes such yew wood highly sought after by woodturners and producers of yew veneer. It is the result of *adventitious growth*.

Vegetative Regeneration

While sexual reproduction has the greatest advantages for the diversity of the genetic pool of a species, vegetative regeneration secures and extends the lifetime of an individual. *Taxus* is capable of quite a number of different methods of vegetative regeneration and – here comes the first surprise – a yew tree can perform them *vigorously at almost any stage* in its lifetime. In other words: age does not seem to weaken this capacity for regrowth.

Great numbers of new shoots can rise from the cambium of branches and trunks, as can so-called 'root suckers' from roots close to the surface (roots above or below ground). In the case of a partly broken crown, vertical shoots may appear on the neighbouring branches and soon fill the gap. New shoots appearing 'out of nowhere' from the bark are called 'adventitious growth', a phenomenon rather rare in the world of conifers, albeit more widespread in angiosperms. The cambium of *Taxus* is actually capable of bringing forth the tissues of a shoot that will burst through the protective layers of the outer bark, and produce green leaves. Often, the entire lower part of a solitary yew tree is covered with such shoots. They may only be there for a few years, to shade the trunk with the living tissues beneath the thin bark from direct sun exposure; or some may develop into substantial (vertical) branches, or even additional trunks. Adventitious growth is not to be confused with dormant buds that lie waiting beneath

Adventitious growth
covers the trunk
and keeps the living
tissue beneath the
thin bark cool.

the bark; adventitious growth, on the cellular level, really does come 'out of nowhere', and is another example of the great plasticity of *Taxus baccata*.

Other observations of the yew's remarkable reproductive abilities include the fact that fallen trees continue to grow as long as enough contact with the root is maintained, with lateral branches becoming new 'leaders' (vertical apical shoots that lead the height increase of a tree). The yew's ability to produce new foliage, branches and leaders anywhere enables it to cope with even severe mechanical damage resulting from storms.[52]

Low-growing branches have a tendency to grow downwards until they touch the ground, whereupon they produce roots. A branch continues to grow sideways (away from the mother trunk), but at

Branch layering.

the point of rooting also produces new (adventitious) shoots that can grow vertically to become leaders for a new tree. We call this cloning these days. In this way, a single yew tree can form a whole grove of dozens of trees, behaviour most people only know from the banyan tree, *Ficus benghalensis*, in subtropical India. Classical writers in Rome mentioned this phenomenon of 'branch layering' as long as 2,000 years ago. It enables an individual tree to make its survival independent of the condition of the wooden structure of the mother tree. Its 'first body' might be destroyed, but the 'tree' lives on in the younger trees. So what is a tree? Phenomena like these force us to revisit our definitions of biological life forms. Is a 'tree' just the process of continuous conversion from living xylem cells to heartwood, after which the tree dies when the trunk disappears? Or is it the root that may bring forth new growth above the surface, like old coppiced linden or ash trees? Or is it the genetic code? Or perhaps it is something else yet? Moreover, the most remarkable yew phenomenon of them all has still to be mentioned: internal roots within the hollow trunks of ancient yew trees.

Internal roots in the ancient hollow yew at St Ursin, France (top left); internal stems
at Kemble, Gloucestershire (top right).
An old internal trunk at Linton, Herefordshire (outer girth 10.06 m, inner trunk
2.1 m, in 1998).

The trunks of very old yews invariably begin to hollow, with the aid of specialized fungi. This slow, centuries-long process also includes the main branches. The hollowing requires a perpetual redistribution of the crown's weight, and the yew meets these needs by laying down more 'primary wood' in the sections that demand it, and by additionally strengthening them with the production of 'secondary wood'. However, the hollowing yew trunk that looks increasingly frail and 'dying' is, unlike in other tree species, not a sign of death at all. For yew it is the first step in a unique transition process that renews the entire tree. In *Taxus*, parts of the cambium at the top of the trunk are capable of developing 'roots' that grow downwards through the hollowing centre of the tree. Sometimes they look rather like branches, but when they reach the ground they penetrate it and take root. Above the surface, the internal 'roots' eventually turn into new trunks themselves, standing inside the hollow old trunk or shell. Since they have been connected to the living tissues (cambium, xylem and phloem) at the top of the old trunk right from the start, they are predestined to progressively take over the role of the main stem, both in terms of sap flow and as a mechanical support structure.

Branch layering and – especially – the ability to produce internal roots and stems are the prime techniques employed by an ancient yew to entirely renew itself physically above the ground, resulting in a 'new' tree in which all parts are by far younger than the living organism itself.

three

Social Yew

꙰

A tree is not a separate being. It interacts and socializes with other trees and plants – ecology speaks of 'plant communities' – and not only interacts *with* its environment, but also *is a part* of this 'environment'. Our thinking is influenced by a strong European tradition of dividing the objects of our interest into ever-smaller units. A more balanced view of nature recognizes the entire ecosphere of planet Earth as one organism, with large ecotopes (oceanic, steppe-lands and forests, among others) as its 'organs', and the animals and plants therein as cells of these organs. A large tree and a small weed alike do not just appear out of nowhere, but are an expression of the entirety of a place. They are linked to terrestrial forces, such as ground and soil type, water courses, earth magnetism, and other force fields and rays, and celestial forces (solar, lunar and stellar), and entangled in many ways with the life forms around them.

We also have to clarify a couple of terms, namely 'competition' and 'ecological strategy'. For most people, 'strategy' is usually associated with the human condition and presupposes a conscious reflection upon one's actions – a consciousness that is not generally accredited to plants, although this term is widely used in ecological literature. In ecological science it can be understood as a dynamic event involving the active participation of the organism in question. The ecological strategy of a species encompasses the entirety of its genetically fixed characteristics (its adaptedness to given environmental conditions), as well as its ability to alter its genetic code within a certain frame to adapt to new conditions (adaptability). The ecological strategy therefore supports the survival of the species.[1]

'Competition' is a term even more loaded with human meaning. At times Darwinism has been used and abused by social and political movements ('survival of the fittest'), which is sad, and irritating for our purposes. In ecology, the situation is not as dramatic. Competition generally denotes a certain rivalry of organisms or species for limited resources, but this does not affect the individual organism as much as it does its population patterns: species mutually limit each other's birth rates and/or growth rates, and/or increase each other's death rates. Competition is considered to be a highly significant motor in forest dynamics – the competition for light was possibly one of the strongest selective factors in the evolution of land plants and the development of upright trunks.[2] Yew, however, takes part in the competition dynamics of the forest only to a very small degree. Its regeneration rate, as well as its girth and biomass increase, are influenced by other species only to a limited extent. To an even lesser degree does yew inhibit the regeneration, growth and death rates of other tree species.[3]

Yew and beech woodland at Sueve Otono, Asturia, Spain.

Cyclamen on yew trunk catching the evening sun at Ortachis, Sardinia.

During the twentieth century, beech (*Fagus*) always out-shaded the yew trees in the understorey (lower tier) and was considered yew's dominant competitor. This picture seemed to be confirmed when the young science of pollen analysis in the 1990s stated that prehistoric yew declines in certain regions paralleled beech invasions in the same areas. That was until someone had the good idea of cross-checking these data with the development of human populations: it then became obvious that these changes in forest structure occurred exactly within the periods of colonization by prehistoric farmers. Beech is a tree that highly benefits from human activity, and could perhaps be regarded as a biological culture indicator. Yew, on the other hand, vanished with man's destruction of old virgin forests, and additionally was especially sought after, as early as the Neolithic period, for its wood qualities. Leaving human activity aside, however, beech woods provide one of the best habitats for yew. Instead of being called a competitor, beech could be described as one of yew's biggest allies, from Ireland across Europe, to Turkey and the Caucasus Mountains.

Another twentieth-century misconception that can no longer be sustained is that of yew being a 'weak competitor'. This came about because during the 1900s yew was disappearing from woodlands across northern Germany and Poland, and at the same time (palaeo-) botanists began to call the yew tree a 'tertiary relic' plant because of its archetypal ancient features. Everyone began to see yew as an artefact from a bygone age with not much of a future. Now we know that the twentieth-century yew decline in Europe was caused by general deforestation and by extraordinary increases of local deer populations (destroying natural rejuvenation), and that yew is far from being 'weak'. A new picture has emerged: *Taxus* is a species that occurs naturally as scattered individuals or in groups or clusters, usually in the understorey of mixed woodlands, it is perfectly adapted to survive in isolated populations, and still occurs in natural stands across the entire physiological range of its habitats – morphologically almost unchanged for 140 million years.[4] If *this* is not success, what is?

The temperate-zone plant communities in which yew is mostly found are forests of pure beech (*Fagus*), or beech mixed with conifers, or mixed oakwoods. Other dominant trees in such woods include ash (*Fraxinus*), sycamore maple (*Acer pseudoplatanus*), fir (*Abies*), spruce (*Picea*), hornbeam (*Carpinus*), linden (*Tilia*) and elm (*Ulmus*). Yew's companions in the understorey are mostly holly (*Ilex*), box (*Buxus*), hazel (*Corylus*) and hawthorn (*Crataegus*), and occasionally also whitebeam (*Sorbus aria*), blackthorn (*Prunus spinosa*) and elder (*Sambucus nigra*). Ground plants in this environment include dog's mercury (*Mercurialis perennis*), wild strawberry (*Fragaria vesca*), ground ivy (*Glechoma hederacea*), ivy (*Hedera helix*), blackberry (*Rubus fruticosus*), common nettle (*Urtica dioica*), and violets (*Viola*). Yew-beechwoods also include wood melick (*Melica uniflora*), woodruff (*Galium odoratum*), cyclamen, and various orchids, while mixed yew-oakwoods yield cowslip (*Primula veris*), peach bell (*Campanula persicifolia*) and bracken (*Pteridium aquilinum*), among others.[5] Yew is not, however, confined to the deep forest: when colonizing the edges of woodland, or even open grassland, yew seedlings find ideal conditions in hawthorn bushes, sometimes blackthorn or other wild shrubs of the rose family, and particularly juniper (*Juniperus*). The latter is the most accommodating nurse plant because it grows in locations most suitable for yew (shallow soils on steep or exposed sites), and its fruits (also those of hawthorn and other shrubs of the rose family) attract birds that will disperse the yew arils beneath them. The yew seedlings find shade and effective protection from herbivores among these thickets, and eventually outgrow their nurse shrubs.[6]

In the Mediterranean, yew also occurs with holm oak (*Quercus ilex*), other oak species and plane (*Platanus*), with an understorey of myrtle (*Myrtus*), laurel (*Laurocerasus*), paradise plant (*Daphne*), box (*Buxus*), hazel (*Corylus*) and others. In Turkey and the Caucasus Mountains, oriental beech (*F. orientalis*) is a significant tree in yew communities. In the ancient mixed yew forest of the Bazara Gorge in Georgia (Caucasus), sweet chestnut (*Castanea sativa*), alder (*Alnus barbata*) and Caucasian hornbeam (*Carpinus caucasia*) are present too.[7]

Yew is an integral part of the climax stage of old beech and oak woodlands. Additionally, because of its pioneering qualities it can help to establish a natural woodland in the first place. Climax woodlands are the ecotopes with the highest biomass production and hence attract a large host of other species to digest that biomass again. Many food chains develop and result in high biodiversity. An example of the yew's part in this process is that it attracts birds; woodlands with yew have higher bird populations than those without yew.

Many other aspects of the mixed yew woodland are almost entirely unexplored, for example yew's complex relationship with beech; how the fungi associated with yew and those associated with beech interact, and how tree roots interact with each other generally, and possibly exchange information and/or substances. There is considerable room for future research here.

four

Ancient Yew

❧

'Are they really that old?' is the question most often asked about the ancient churchyard yews in Britain. Since the 1990s the fact that many of those big, chunky, archetypal trees might be a millennium old, or even much more, has slowly risen to public awareness. One thousand years is a huge time span, and a symbolic one at that. A beech, for example, only lives for a quarter of that time, and that is still three times more than our own life span. Yet no village would pride itself, and no postcard would be worth printing, if the venerated tree in question were not at least 1,000 years old – 800 or 900 years simply would not do. With trees, one has to accept that '1,000' does not relate to tree-ring analysis (dendrochronology), but is an emotional term and a badge of honour. In a way that is good enough if it helps to protect the ancient tree – but often it does the opposite. The ages of many yew trees were indeed vastly exaggerated until Victorian times. Since the end of the 1800s, incredulous scientists have been careful to distance themselves from that and hence have been overcautious in crediting old age to any yew tree. The oldest tree among dozens of one-thousand-year-old oak trees in Germany proved to be some 560 years old. European trees that undoubtedly exceed that magical mark are a linden (lime) and a few coppiced ash and linden trees in Britain and Germany.

When it comes to real counting, there are trees that are even older than that, of course. The Americans are fortunate to have redwoods, which can live for more than a millennium. The *Guinness Book of Records'*

Left to right: Yew at 50 years, spruce at 80 years (± 10 years), beech at 90 years, yew at 190 years (± 10 years), Paterzell, Bavaria.

holder of the oldest tree accolade is a bristlecone pine (*Pinus longaeva*) nicknamed 'Prometheus', which in 1964 showed 4,844 rings in a cross-section. It was the oldest proven non-cloned living thing on Earth; ironically it was cut down in the process of obtaining these data. We have more refined tools for dendrochronology today, although yew wood is so hard that three out of four drill parts break when holes are drilled into a tree. However, the main problem for age estimates is that the trunks of mature yews begin to hollow from an age of about 500 years (but sometimes only 300 years). You cannot count tree rings when there is no wood in the first place. In other species this kind of rot is a sure sign of general decay that signals old age and approaching death, but *Taxus* can live for countless centuries with a hollow trunk. It is 'in control' of the hollowing process, and this is part of its survival strategy.

Yew does not reveal its secrets easily, if at all. With no wood, no physical matter being as old as the tree itself (which also renders radio-carbon dating useless), no one can apply an exact number of years to an ancient yew. In order to get some idea of an age bracket we need to take an in-depth look into the growth rates and life stages of trees.

Growth Rates

Generally, trees in the temperate zone have three phases of life. In each of these phases the growth rates (girth increase, correlated to the thickness of annual rings) are different.

1 The 'formative period' of vigorous growth, during which the increase of trunk girth reflects the increasing crown size.

2 The 'mature state', when the optimum crown size is reached (in most temperate species after 40–100 years) and the annual increment of new wood (the total mass of wood that the tree is making each year) stabilizes. This implies, however, that the annual rings become increasingly thinner as the trunk circumference increases: a 'constant annual increment' (CAI) is spread over an increasing surface area.

3 'Senescence', when the tree has outgrown its limits of feeding itself. Parts of the crown die back and hence reduce the photo-synthesizing foliage, resulting in a constant decrease in annual wood production and in annual ring width. When the mean annual ring width of the trunk falls below 0.5 mm, most tree species die in due course.[1] Only *Juniperus* and *Taxus* (and to a certain extent *Pinus*) can survive long stretches of time with much less growth than that. In fact, they can even produce rings so narrow that they remain invisible to the naked human eye.

Extremely slow growth occurs in very difficult habitats, the prime example being vertical rock cliffs with northern exposure: no soil, constant dehydrating high winds and little sun. Growing under such circumstances, a juniper (*Juniperus phoenicea*) from the Verdon Gorge, France, took 1,140 years to produce only 8 cm (approx. 3¼ in) of trunk radius, equalling an average ring width of just over 0.06 mm.[2] An extraordinary dead-wood sample from a yew at Whitbarrow Scar, Cumbria, revealed 220 rings in about 16 mm (¾ in) radius. That is an average ring width of 0.0073 mm, so it takes more than thirteen years to produce 1 mm of radius, 349 years to produce 25.4 mm (1 in). Such trees are botanical miracles, each producing a total woody biomass of well below 0.1 g on annual average.[3] With some tree rings only being one cell layer thick, we can additionally expect scattered single years when the tree does not put on anything at all. It can safely be assumed that these trees are among the slowest-growing woody plants on Earth.

These are, however, the extremes. In 'normal' conditions yews grow much more quickly, but still only at about half the rate of other forest trees like fir, spruce, pine and the hardwoods. A rule of thumb for the age estimate of trees is: for trees in the open, 25.4 mm (1 in) girth, equivalent to about 4-mm ring width, represents one year of lifetime; in dense forests trees grow at half that (25.4 mm/1 in girth in two years, equalling 2 mm annual radius). The values should be halved for young yews.

Dr Andy K. Moir and Toby Hindson of the Ancient Yew Group (AYG) recently came to this same rule of thumb independently of one another: broadly speaking the average mature yew increases girth at 1 cm (½ in) each year. This rule of thumb applies to young and straight forest trees, but yews are often multi-stemmed, twisted and irregular, and have fluted trunks. Yew tree rings do not necessarily grow concentrically outwards from the pith, equally in all directions (due to a slanting trunk, for example). Although a yew generally strives to produce wood as evenly as possible (not growing much faster in good years, but rather storing reserves for poor years to maintain the growth rate), there are vast differences in the response range in different locations, and also in the genotypes of the trees themselves. Hence we know yew avenues where neighbouring trees possess the same age but astonishingly different size. At Monnington Walk in Herefordshire, for example, 42 yews planted in 1628 had, by 2003, varying girths from 1.47 m to 4.42 m (4 ft 11 in–14 ft 9 in).[4]

In general, the rate of girth increment of *Taxus* in the formative years culminates at an age of around 110–120 years, while the rate of height increment ends even later at about 150–160 years; both rates culminate much later than those of all other trees.[5] On the other hand, *Taxus* slows down its girth increase considerably in older age, which in age estimation somewhat balances the prolonged formative period of faster growth. Further complexity is added by the fact that yew is also able to:

> return to formative (i.e. vigorous) rates of growth at almost any stage in its very long life. It may be stimulated by a boost of plant food from branch layering, or by vigorous regeneration after catastrophic damage,[6]

or simply by the disappearance of other trees shading it.

Many tree experts have avoided the subject of estimating the ages of yew trees. It has been safer to quote someone from the past (a strength and weakness of science), but this does not exactly make for cutting-edge science. We desperately need accurate information because the lives of the trees are at stake. Decision makers in politics, faiths, communities, utilities services regulation (for example water and drainage) and the economy need substantiated 'facts'. Our understanding of *Taxus* is still a map with large white spaces. As mentioned in the description of the young yew sapling – if we cannot even say whether a 2 m (6½ ft) tall forest yew is 20 or 60 years old, how could anyone possibly estimate the age of an ancient yew with a girth of 6 m (20 ft) or even 11 m (36 ft)?

Life Stages

Yew does not fit into the framework of the three phases of tree life as used by forestry commissions in different countries. A more suitable model was put forward by Toby Hindson in 2000.[7] His proposal of seven instead of three life stages for *Taxus baccata* is the first to fully acknowledge the complicated growth rhythms of this species – and most significantly the fact that *Taxus* does not have to die after stage three, but undergoes a full process of self-renewal through the application of

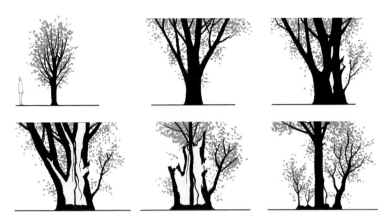

Diagram of six of the seven life stages of yew (seedling stage not shown).

the hollowing and restructuring of the trunk, and additionally the growth of internal roots and internal stems.

STAGE 1 *The seedling* From germination; during the first few years the rate of girth increment is slow.

STAGE 2 *The juvenile* The tree has a fast growth rate; annual rings are usually a few millimetres thick.

STAGE 3 *The solid tree* Full size is reached and the tree is in its prime; the core is intact. The amount of wood produced each year stabilizes, which means, however, that with the increase in girth the actual ring width decreases accordingly, so John White's model of Constant Annual Increment (CAI) applies when the age of a yew is being considered.

STAGE 4 *Hollowing* Trunk girth continues to increase, but very slowly. Core rot begins inside the trunk, but the trunk and crown remain functional for a long time to come. As more and more of the heart-wood disappears, weight pressure on the outer trunk areas, namely the sapwood, increases. Because the sapwood is not designed to cope with compression, the tree begins to put down new growth ('secondary growth') in the sections under stress, and with increasing vigour. The annual girth increment therefore rises, but if internal stems develop a growing percentage of cambium activity is transferred to them and increased growth in the lower bole may not be fully apparent.

STAGE 5 *The hollow tree* Although (almost) fully hollowed out, the trunk and supporting structures maintain a full crown. The girth increment rate remains high, particularly at the base of the trunk, to redistribute weight pressures. In the last phase of this stage, the tall, empty cone of the trunk cannot support itself any more and begins to collapse, loosening parts of the canopy as well. If one or more internal stems exist, they begin to dominate xylem tube production; a shift that can lower the girth increase of the outer trunk significantly, even to a standstill.

STAGE 6 *The shell* The short, hollow tube has little canopy and hence little weight to support. Fast wood production is not required any more (and would not be possible anyway with such reduced foliage). Old trunk growth slows down considerably. If one or more internal stems exist, they feed branches that eventually make up a 'new' tree.

STAGE 7 *The ring* In the final stage of the cycle, (semi)circles of vertical fragments of the old shell may begin to take the appearance of independent trees – though most probably continuing to share the same root system and hence be one tree – with primary and secondary wood slowly giving their trunks a round, 'finished' look. If the old shell disappears completely, new shoots may appear from the stump or root system. In any case, the life of the tree continues, making it impossible for us to determine an end or beginning of its life, let alone its age. As the venerable Alan Mitchell (1922–1995), founder of the Tree Register of the British Isles, said: 'There is no theoretical end for this tree, no need for it to die.'[8]

Of course, only a minority of individual yew trees succeed in living the species' full potential, and most die along the way. Yet the numbers are heart-warming: for Britain, the Ancient Yew Group (AYG) data-base has listed 950 trees in the category 'veteran' with a girth of 4.9 m (16 ft 9 in) and more, and 360 trees in the category 'ancient' with a girth of 7 m (23 ft) or more (as of August 2013). The age brackets are 500 to 1,200 years for the 'veterans', and more than 800 years, no upper limit, for the 'ancients'. These are very conservative estimates when compared with the formulae used by the Forestry Commission (Tabbush and White). Tabbush's churchyard formula (tree age = girth^2/310) estimates a yew with 7 m (23 ft) girth at 1,580 years of age.

The life stages described above need to be considered when measuring an ancient yew tree for age estimation. At the same given girth, a hollowing tree is probably older than one with a dense, compact trunk. A completely hollow shell is older than that, but not as old as a group of fragments. Beyond that a single fragment may have become enclosed in secondary growth and appear as a rounded young trunk. Or an ancient tree may have entirely disappeared above ground, and the regrowth from its (still living) root might be mistaken for a group of young trees; in such cases, only the circular shape of the whole group may indicate that this is indeed an ancient tree. Another aspect to consider in age estimation is that trees on poor soil or solid rock grow much more slowly than those with more favourable growing conditions.

There are still books and articles around which state that *Taxus* is not 'proven' to be able to live beyond, or even reach, one millennium. Little do their authors know that the ability of *Taxus* to live longer than a millennium is not questioned in the international scientific community outside Britain. For example, a dendrochronological study from the Black Sea region in northern Turkey had the rare luck of examining an unbroken sequence of 426 years, from 1572 to 1998. The probe shows an average annual growth rate of 0.461-mm ring width, which even in single years hardly ever ventures into the 1 mm region. It was taken from one of the 'monumental yews' of Turkey with a trunk radius of 110 cm (44 in). Assuming the same average growth rate for the rest of its lifetime, the age of the tree would be

Regrowth from root, Ystrad Aeron, Ceredigion (Wales).

A hollow shell at Dunsfold, Surrey.

Fragments of a shell, Molash, Kent.

about 2,380 years.[9] Other monumental yews in northern Turkey (Alapli Nature Reserve) reach heights of around 20 m (67 ft). The tree with the second-largest girth measures 7.96 m (26 ft), the tree with the largest one 9.20 m (30 ft). At the aforementioned growth rate they would have ages of about 2,740 and 3,170 years, respectively. Another sample from a monumental yew, this one from dense forest in the Khosta Nature Reserve in the western Caucasus Mountains, Russia, has 113 rings in 33.1 mm (1¼ in). At this rate, the trunk's radius of about 50 cm (20 in) would have needed some 1,660 years to grow.[10] One might allow ±5 per cent for variation in these examples, or even ten or twenty, but no mathematical acrobatics could bring the estimates for such trees below or even near the 1,000-year threshold that seems to be so difficult for some to believe, for whatever reasons.

Ancient yew on the rocks. Sardinia.

Rounding fragments
in Sardinia.

There is more evidence from Russia: Professor Mikhail Pridnya, leading botanist and curator of the western Caucasian nature reserves (southwestern Russia), states about *Taxus* that:

> from living individuals nearby Khosta exceeding a diameter of 2 meters, one knows that they can exceed an age of 3,000 years [referring to the number of rings of sample trunks with similar diameter].

Pridnya also reports a circular, cross-cut disc of a yew trunk with just over 1,000 rings in a just over 50-cm (20-in) radius, and still with a completely intact core. Tragically, this evidence was destroyed by a fire at the Sochi State Museum in 1970.[11] Finally, some news from Britain: in 2004, dendrochronologist Dr Moir examined the famous Borrowdale Yews in Cumbria. His conclusion was that one of the trees – ironically the one with the smallest girth – is aged around 1,400 years.[12]

All in all, we are at the beginning of a *new* understanding of how yews age. Girth – in fact size in general – is not as reliable a factor as we thought. Each yew site has to be assessed on its own merits. Given that the yew of smallest girth at Borrowdale is the oldest, this suggests that the biggest yew in any yew grove may not be the oldest one. The biggest oak in an oak group is the oldest, as is the biggest beech in a beech grove, but not so the yew. The yew confounds us, and demands that we ask again and again: how can this be so? How can a tree be so different from any other kind of tree? This is another reason why yews should be protected – precisely because *we do not know exactly what they are yet*. The more we discover, the more we find out how precious and priceless and irreplaceable they are. If anything, yew trees deserve the designation 'Green Monuments', and the full protection that would follow with it – but to achieve that they require more research.

In Britain, two widespread misconceptions have confused the age discussion more than anything else. For one, there is the common mistake of interpreting internal stems simply as young trees. A tree at Ninfield, Sussex, now consists of a whole group of young internal stems grown while the old shell finally dropped away during the course of the twentieth century.[13] Because this is a time-consuming process, it may be much older than the fragments of the tree at Molash in Kent. Similarly, the sacred yew at Jirobei, Japan, is an ancient tree that consists entirely of exposed internal stems, although it looks incredibly young and vigorous. A similar misjudgement can arise at the sight of regrowth from an ancient root if there are no more shell fragments left to indicate the original girth; in such cases, the peculiar circular shape of the group may be the only indicator. In other yews, the internal growth is monocormic and produces a single internal trunk. In trees like those at Linton, Herefordshire, and the oldest yew at Bettws Newydd, Monmouthshire, the internal trunk looks awe-inspiring and makes it easier to imagine how the growth of living

Dense group of internal stems, with the old shell entirely gone. Ninfield, Sussex.

tissues (and hence girth) has long begun to shift from the old shell to the new trunk inside the hollow.

Most of all, the interpretation of yew trees with multiple trunks as 'fused trunks',[14] has mislead many researchers, the argument being that the tree has 'cheated' and is not as old as the overall girth would suggest because two or more trees have 'fused'. A fusion of wood growth can indeed be observed when branches of the same tree grow close and finally merge. This may happen from time to time with neighbouring independent trees, too. However, to state that half-a-dozen close-standing trees – with different genders – communicate with each other in order to 'merge' and agree on one sex is simply botanical nonsense. The truth is, a multitude of leaders is a natural part of the appearance of *Taxus* from an early age on. With up to a third of yew seedlings already displaying a delayed apical shoot (the leader at the very top of the tree) and its substitution by three to six competing vertical shoots – a percentage that steadily increases because of browsing damage – it is no wonder that mature trees develop multiple trunks. Because the ancient yew at Tandridge, Surrey, had been under lasting 'suspicion' of trunk fusion, I commissioned a DNA test in 2004, sampling leaf buds from the two main trunks at the opposite ends of

Competing apical shoots in a yew seedling.

Ancient yew at Tandridge, Surrey (girth 10.07 m in 1999).

An ancient yew in the Russian Caucasus.

the elongated base. The results proved that the DNA in the different parts of the tree was identical. The distant trunks of the ancient yew at Tandridge are not fused but belong to *one* tree.[15]

Old age is not a thing that 'just happens', but is an integral part of the survival strategy of some species. In *Taxus baccata* the most outstanding characteristics are vitally linked with each other and provide the potential for an extraordinarily long lifespan. They include slow growth, effective storage of resources, toxicity and high resistance of the organs, high adaptability (leading to general high stress tolerance), low photosynthesis performance, the extraordinarily fast response of the stomata, immense potential for regeneration (adventitious growth, branch layering), and the creation of internal roots in hollowing trunks. Ecologically, all these are safety mechanisms and they make possible a yew's survival in the most diverse ecological conditions.[16] The extremely advanced age that *Taxus* can reach provides it with the ability to rejuvenate in especially favourable periods in between large interims.[17] The ecological strategy of the genus differs entirely from that of any other tree species in the temperate zone. Its resultant high life expectancy is a proof of the success of this strategy.

five

Hospitable Yew

༺

For a poisonous tree, the yew attracts a surprising host of wildlife. It is mostly the juicy and nutritious arils that offer nourishment to a range of birds and various mammals. The foliage, however toxic, seems to be cherished by browsing deer, rabbits and hares, while the multitude of crevices in old yew trees offer perfect home-making conditions for wild bees, owls and bats.

Fungi

Due to its toxicity, yew is protected from the majority of plant parasites and also from extensive browsing by animals. However, yew populations, particularly their seedlings and saplings, do suffer from browsing damage, particularly by deer. Birds and some mammals, on the other hand, eat the non-toxic, fleshy arils and help to disperse the seeds contained therein.

There are no reports about bacterial infections in *Taxus*. Most fungi stay away, too. Yew is not attacked by the common dry rot fungus (*Serpula lacrymans*) and is also very resistant to honey fungus (*Armillaria* spp.),[1] a mushroom genus that produces the largest fungal underground networks known and lives on nutrients from decaying wood as well as from the *living* roots of hardwood trees and conifers alike. *Armillaria* can be a fatal threat to trees, but there are no authenticated cases of yew death due to the widespread honey fungus. The only known fatal disease of yew in Britain (1994) is an infection with the root pathogen *Phytophthora*,[2] a genus that has in recent years attracted much attention for attacking various shrubs and trees like larches, oaks, maples and chestnuts. In a yew wood in Poland, the presence of the pathogenic fungus *Nectria radicicola* in the soil seems to kill yew seedlings. In a yew stand in Switzerland (Fürstenwald, near Chur, Canton Grisons), one in four yew trees manifests widespread stem canker, thought to be caused by the golden spreading polypore (*Phellinus chrysoloma*), a fungus that also attacks living spruce, fir and larch trees (but never pine). It enters the heartwood via broken branches or other deep wounds, and attacks the cambium. It later spreads into the living sapwood, and if the decay is faster than the new tree growth it reaches the bark surface, where cankers develop as a consequence. The living part of the cambium is increasingly pushed away from the bark and ceases to be able to seal the wound with wound material (callus). However, the fungal growth in yew is very slow; in this location the trees have been fighting the infection for some 60 years, and some have managed to isolate and constrain the infection.[3] Altogether, 258 fungus and slime-mould species have been identified so far on *Taxus*

The sulphur bracket (*Laetiporus sulphureus*) is an important ally for the yew.

83

baccata or on the soil beneath yew trees. This is not many if we consider that beech and oak are host to about 2,200 species each.[4]

It needs to be added that fungal growth in wood is strongly bound to the permeability of the wood, which allows the hyphae of a fungus to penetrate, or prevents them from doing so. Since the permeability of yew heartwood is extremely low – much lower than that in any other European tree – the high fungal resistance of *Taxus* probably owes more to the physical density of its wood than to its infamous toxicity.[5]

One species of fungus plays a crucial part in the life cycle of yew. The decay (and complete removal) of the old heartwood necessary for the hollowing process of the trunk and main branches of old yew trees is most commonly performed by the sulphur bracket *Laetiporus sulphureus*. This is a very unusual form of symbiosis and it is entirely unknown how tree and fungus 'communicate' which parts of the tree are ready for consumption. There is room for future research here.

Insects

Yew is equally not pestered by insects. There are only three species of note, two of them being mites. The yew big bud mite (*Cecidophyopsis psilaspis*) causes abnormal elongation and swelling of the bud scales, which leads to extensive and chronic bud mortality throughout the canopy and thereby an irregular branching pattern. Most importantly, its annual return can cause the loss of the apical shoot in seedlings and saplings. Yew is able to balance that with raising one or more upper side shoots to take its place, but this often results in a young tree with more than one leader, which then grows into a polycormic (multi-trunked) tree. This little insect therefore contributes to the scarcity of tall monocormic yews.[6]

Another mite, *Eriophyes psilaspis*, causes tumour-like growths and deformations as well as discolouration of leaves and buds. In the long run, leaf buds and male flowers dry up and fall off. Most prominent, however, and endemic to yew, is the yew gall midge (*Taxomyia taxi*), the cause of the 'artichoke' galls so often seen on yews in Europe (but not in America and Japan). The gall is a dense needle cluster formed by the tree in response to stimulation by the newly hatched larva of the insect. Following its pupa stage the adult insect emerges from the gall after either one or two years. The yew gall midge is not a dangerous 'parasite', but a specialized herbivore whose activities have little effect on the overall growth of the affected yew trees. Any healthy tree can tolerate the small percentage of loss of single shoots. The gall-midge populations never become epidemic, and are kept in balance by the effect of two parasites that prey on the gall-midge larvae.[7]

Among the harmless insects stopping by for a snack are the caterpillars of two moths, the red-barred tortrix (*Ditula angustiorana*) and *Blastobasis lignea*, which feed on yew leaves (including gall leaves and gall-midge larvae). They themselves are prey to birds, especially tits. Furthermore, the larvae of the house longhorned beetle (*Hylotrupes bajulus*) and deathwatch beetle (*Xestobium rufovillosum*) attack the sapwood of yew. A more dangerous visitor is the black vine weevil (*Otiorhynchus sulcatus*), a beetle that 'ringbarks' young shoots all around the stem, causing them to turn red, wither and die. It also attacks the roots of seedlings as well as their apical buds, further adding to the predominance of multi-stemmed (and later multi-trunked) yews.[8] Ants visit yew to eat the sweet pulp of fallen arils, thereby exposing the seeds and improving seed germination to a humble extent. Last but not least, wild honeybees (*Apis mellifica*) find perfect nest-building conditions inside hollow yews. In the distant past, bee keeping was not a domestic activity confined to hives. Instead, the honey collector would get the combs from wild bees nesting in caves or in the crevices of trees.

Birds

The greatest hospitality yew offers is to birds: great nesting opportunities, dense shelter and an abundance of delicious, nutritious red fruits. At least eighteen species of bird eat the arils, and they are the

Thrushes, like this mistle thrush, are the main seed dispersers of yew trees.

This robin came for a meal in the middle of winter.

Left: Finches like this hawfinch are the dominant yew seed predators.
Right: The nuthatch is a seed predator that occasionally plants new yew trees by accident.

main agents of yew seed dispersal.[9] They eat the arils with the seeds, but later disgorge the seeds or pass them intact through their digestive tracts. This removes the fleshy aril that would otherwise inhibit germination. Yew and birds are made for each other. It is on birds' wings that new yew generations travel long distances, reaching isolated and sometimes inaccessible locations such as steep cliff faces and walls. In Culmstock, Devon, a yew tree grows on a church tower. However, more seeds germinate beneath a birds' resting places, for example under tall fir trees and broadleaves, or in the secure shelter of juniper, hawthorn or blackthorn shrubs, whereby yew might slowly colonize open spaces outside a forest.

The four most dominant seed dispersers, and hence the most important allies of yew, are starling and three members of the thrush family: song thrush, blackbird and mistle thrush. Studies in the British Isles and Germany have shown that their levels of aril consumption are followed by those of three more aril-eating thrushes, fieldfare, redwing and ring ouzel, as well as those of robin, blackcap, waxwing, jay and pheasant. Other birds that eat arils are wagtails and spotted nutcrackers. Among all of these, song thrush is the biggest aril eater, with arils constituting about a quarter of its autumn diet. For mistle thrush and starling, arils make up 16 and 18 per cent of their food intake, respectively. In a single meal, a mistle thrush may eat as many as twenty arils, a fieldfare even up to thirty, but generally the birds' meals are smaller, amounting to about eight to twelve arils a visit. This relatively small aril intake suits the tree, because there is no advantage for seed dispersal if the droppings of birds create dense little clusters of too many seedlings. After a yew meal, birds need to drink frequently, and can be observed washing their bills. The extent of the yew–bird relationship was emphasized by a painstaking survey of the Killarney woodland in Ireland in 1975 and 1976, when the number of arils was estimated at 2.6 and 6.2 million arils per square mile, respectively. This equals about 96 and 308 kg (212 and 679 lb) of arils per square metre, with a total energy content of 0.6 and 1.9 billion calories. The birds ate an estimated 35 per cent and 43 per cent per cent of the weight of the arils in each of the two years.[10] It is no surprise, then, that woodlands rich in yew trees attract more birds than areas without yews.

The intimate relationship of yew and birds is bound to be old, and in fact it can be dated to the Jurassic period. The predecessor of all birds, *Archaeopteryx*, a winged and feathered small dinosaur, is fossilized in strata 159 to 144 million years old. *Taxus jurassica* is 140 million years old, and it seems probable that the arils of early yews would have been eaten by some of the earliest bird species.

As well as the seed dispersers, there are birds that do not eat the juicy pulp but go for the seed itself: these seed predators crack open the shell and eat the embryo. The main yew-seed predator by far is the greenfinch, but birds such as great tit, bullfinch, hawfinch, nuthatch, green woodpecker and great spotted woodpecker also eat the seeds.

Members of the tit family are interesting yew visitors. In order to open the seed to access the embryo, they employ a technique that is shared with woodpeckers and nuthatches: they wedge the seed in a crack in the yew bark to stabilize it, then hammer it open with their beak. Additionally, tits are able to firmly fix the seed with their feet, provided they are on a horizontal surface. Apart from eating tree fruits (also acorns, beechnuts, haws and ash keys), tits hunt insects in the canopies of trees. A *Taxus* canopy has only a limited insect life to offer, but its peeling bark holds moderate populations of small spiders that attract tits.[11] However, the overall impact of the seed predators on yew rejuvenation is quite small compared with that of the seed dispersers.

Woodpeckers, too, have their own story in relation to yew. In various European countries as well as in the USA (southwestern Oregon), many woodland yews bear strange marks: horizontal rows or complete rings of small, evenly spaced holes around the trunk. The holes are usually 3–8 mm ($^2/_{16}$–$^5/_{16}$ in) in diameter, while the distance between the horizontal rings measures about 9–11 cm (3½–4 in). The holes are deep enough to damage the living tissues beneath the bark and thus impair the production of new wood, the water transport and especially the sap transport of a tree. A few such yews have even died of this.[12] The phenomenon was first reported in the 1990s, but there are still no eyewitnesses to the cause. It is assumed, however, that the work is done by certain species of woodpecker that are known to sometimes drill holes into the bark of selected trees (oak, linden, beech, pine, larch, spruce and wild service tree) to drink some sap, and to then leave them to serve as 'community feeding stations'. Other birds, mammals and insects visit the holes to consume the sap and inner bark, and to glean associated insects. The woodpeckers can create vast numbers of holes – on some single trees not just hundreds, but thousands. There is still no explanation as to why they suddenly create more than a few single holes, why they should single out the rare yew trees for this activity or why the holes in some trees do not even penetrate deeply enough to reach the living tissue. The woodpeckers' behaviour could be an instinctive act of self-medication, involving the use of yews' toxicity to get rid of parasites in their digestive tracts – a theory that has also been put forward in relation to deer browsing yew foliage.[13]

Animal predators rarely visit yew. The great numbers of birds and small mammals in the vicinity of yew occasionally attract hawks and buzzards. Crows and magpies are even less interested in the culinary lures that yew might have to offer, but sometimes they take up residence and overwinter in a yew tree. Nocturnal predators in Europe, particularly the common barn owl and tawny owl, are interested in the mice and other rodents that forage on the seeds. The tawny owl is now rarely seen in woodlands because of the lack of suitable nesting holes in the straight trunks of commercial tree plantations. The disappearance of old trees, particularly yews, in many forests has made life harder for owls.

Mammals

While most birds stick to the arils, mammals – namely certain rodents and hoofed animals – are more of a burden for yew populations because they browse the foliage. Mice and voles do not eat the green parts,[14] but in autumn and winter yew seeds can become their main diet. In Co. Durham, northeast England, 60 per cent of seed fall has been reported to be hijacked by rodents; in the Andalusian highlands in southeast Spain, the figure is as high as 87 per cent. In all fairness, it needs to be said that rodents often stash more seeds than they eventually eat, which sometimes results in close groups of a dozen seedlings on the forest floor. Some voles prey on yew roots as well, and seedlings up to about 2 m (7 ft) in height have reportedly been killed by this activity.[15]

The European red squirrel eats the yew fruit whole. So does the grey squirrel, regurgitating the seed later.[16] While grey squirrels surely play a balanced role in the North American ecosystems (coniferous forests), where they are native, they cause a lot of damage to forests in the UK, where they were introduced in the late nineteenth/ early twentieth centuries. They browse on the leaves and twigs of many trees, and even strip the bark of trees such as hornbeam, beech, birch, willow, Scots pine, sycamore and also yew. Grey squirrels also

In Europe as well as in Japan, the red squirrel is a natural guest when the yew tree bears fruit.

rob birds' nests (and incidentally those of red squirrels, too), particularly the first nests of mistle thrush, after the young have hatched.[17]

Hares and rabbits regularly browse on yew, which can drastically affect yew rejuvenation. Yew is tolerant of repeated pruning, though, and established young trees are able to continue to (re)grow even under (moderate) browsing pressure. In an extreme case, one small yew on the South Downs was heavily visited by rabbits over the years, and was found to be just 18 cm (7 in) tall at an age of about 55 years.[18] On the other hand, the young yew woods in the South Downs, for example, were able to establish themselves in the eighteenth century as a result of an outbreak of myxomatosis (a fatal viral disease of rabbits).[19]

The most severe browsing damage is done by deer. The presence of roe deer (*Capreolus capreolus*) is the main factor inhibiting successful yew regeneration in many countries. Deer browse intensively from the ground to whatever height their necks can reach, generally about 1.35 m (4 ft 5 in). This is particularly harmful because when coming upon a yew woodland, deer browse at the wood's edge – exactly where yew rejuvenation predominantly takes place. Because deer have no incisors in the upper jaw, food is usually torn rather than cut (as in the case of hare and rabbit), so yew seedlings and saplings get entirely destroyed right down to and including their roots. Additionally, male roe deer cause bark damage when they rub off the velvet skin from their annual antler regrowth each summer. Fallow deer (*Dama dama*) cause damage, too, but are not as common as roe deer. In North America, moose occasionally browse yew, as do caribou, but their distribution range hardly touches the northern fringes of the yew's.

The soft yew foliage is additionally attractive to domestic animals such as sheep, goats and sometimes even cattle. Its poisonous properties do not ward off mammals as successfully as they do fungi and insects. Interestingly, wild animals seem to be able to browse yew without poisoning themselves, while domestic animals can be seriously harmed and even killed.

Other visitors who brush up their diets with the help of yew include badger and wild boar, which eat arils off the ground, and edible dormouse and forest dormouse, which pick them from the trees. In the Moroccan mountains, the arils are eaten by wild monkeys (Barbary macaques).[20]

Among the carnivores visiting yew are stoats (ermines) and weasels (*Mustela* sp.) as well as martens (*Martes martes*), which eat yew arils and distribute the seeds with their faeces. Even brown bear (*Ursus arctos*, in America the grizzly) has yew arils on its diet plan; all the better if honeybees should live in the same yew tree. Red fox deserves special mention here. Not only does it enjoy meals of up to two pounds of arils that later lead to the dropping of an excremental red 'haggis' that can contain over 200 yew seeds, but it also visits yew woods to hunt small rodents, rabbits and hares and thus helps keep the tree damage at moderate levels. More importantly, foxes help to keep the deer populations down, which is tremendously beneficial for the rejuvenation of yew (and other forest trees). The main natural deer hunter, however, is wolf, the largest dog-like carnivore. In their hunting activities wolf packs perform an important natural function in controlling the numbers of large herbivores – which is why a proverb from Central Europe states 'Where the wolf walks, the forest grows'.[21] After its long extinction in many countries, the present gradual return of the wolf to Central Europe can only be welcomed by foresters and everybody who cares for trees and woodlands. Until its full return, here is a secret tip from a Bavarian yew-wood forester:

> Dog-walkers letting their dogs run free can help yew rejuvenation because deer avoid to roam where they smell dog (or human). Obviously, do not unleash your pet during the hunting season!

A genus of omnivore that has a tremendous impact on the populations of species around it is man (*Homo* ssp.). The first two-legged creature to encounter yew was probably *Homo ergaster*, who left Africa via the Levante and reached the southern Caucasus Mountains, where he developed into *Homo georgicus* between 1.9 and 1.8 million years ago. The two waves of the first hominid colonization of Europe – by *Homo antecessor* about 1.2 million years ago, and by *Homo heidelbergensis* about 600,000 years ago – will have made use of cave dwellings. Since about 70 per cent of the well-developed caves in the world are formed of limestone[22] – the very rock that provides the favourite subsoil for *Taxus* worldwide – yew can be assumed to have been a continuous 'neighbour' of early hominids in Europe.

The yew spear from Clacton-on-Sea in Essex was for almost a century known as 'the world's oldest artefact of wood'.[23] It was discovered in 1911 with flintstone artefacts and animal bones in strata belonging to the second-last interglacial period, the Hoxnian Stage, between 300,000 and 200,000 years ago. The maker of the Clacton spear was probably *Homo heidelbergensis*. (This is only the second oldest artefact now, because in 1994–5 six short wooden spears were found in Germany, one of pine and five of spruce, which are about 320,000 years old.) Later, 200,000 years ago, the Neanderthal developed in Europe, and the now third-oldest wooden artefact in the world is a Neanderthal yew spear found in the ribs of a straight-tusked mammoth (*Hespero-loxodon antiquus*). This artefact dates from the last interglacial period, the early Eemian interglacial, between 128,000 and 115,000 years ago. During this time *Taxus* distribution was significant, its pollen representing up to 20 per cent of all tree pollen precipitation.[24] The Eemian was sparsely populated with Neanderthals and rich in yew. The final migration of our own species, *Homo sapiens*, from Africa to Europe occurred about 45,000 years ago, again via the Levante, Anatolia and the Balkans. Limestone caves, some of them with yew in the vicinity, were one of man's principal shelters for the remainder of the Palaeolithic period.

Ancient yew at Stanford Bishop, Herefordshire (girth 6.94 m in 2012).

This mountain yew in the Supramonte region in Sardinia (*c.* 1,300 m altitude) is a relic of an ancient forest.

From the viewpoint of yew, *Homo sapiens* was an unusual creature. It was the first that did not only come to the trees for food (arils) or shelter, or to pick a few twigs for medicinal purposes; the two-legged creature also came to collect wood to make tools and hunting bows and spears, or to use as scraps for firewood. When humans learned to build homes they began to come more specifically for wood, killing whole trees for the bigger pieces they needed. On the other hand, humans were the first animals that would not just destroy plants and trees, but were also able to *care* for them – to protect, tend, nurse and water them as if they were their own children. Indeed, for yew the most complex relationship on Earth had begun.

six

Poisonous Yew

All parts of the yew apart from the ripe red aril are poisonous to human beings and other mammals. They contain various amounts of toxic substances, mainly alkaloids. These so-called taxines are a mixture of at least eleven substances, of which the most detrimental to human and animal health is taxine B. The taxine content in leaves varies with the seasons, being about four times higher in the winter (2 per cent) than during summer (0.5 per cent), but leaves with 3 or even 4 per cent taxine content have also been found. The seeds inside the wooden shells contain less taxine than leaf tissue, usually about 0.33 per cent. A third of the overall taxine content in leaves and seeds is taxine B.

After the consumption of yew matter such as foliage, taxine B is rapidly absorbed by the digestive tracts of humans and other mammals. It strongly irritates the digestive tract and affects the nervous system and liver. Its chief action is against the cardiac muscles, resulting in heart failure and death. The personal experience of yew poisoning would be as follows: 30 to 90 minutes after intake vomiting occurs, with intense internal pains, diarrhoea with colicky pain, dizziness and numbness. Breathing speeds up at first, but then becomes continuously slower and shallower. Circulatory disorders, and possibly suffocation cramps, are followed by collapse, fading consciousness and coma. Paralysis of the heart and the breathing apparatus finally leads to death – which occurs within 24 hours, but sometimes in as little as one and a half hours. The global average rate of yew deaths for humans is as low as one case every 3.3 years, and so far all the deaths have been deliberate (suicides).[1]

First aid for a case of yew poisoning involves calling an ambulance, inducing vomiting, and providing 10 g of carbon powder and a dose of sodium sulphate. Survivors of serious yew poisoning are likely to experience long-standing excessive urine production (diuresis), corresponding and considerable hypokalemia, a condition of low potassium levels, resulting in general weakness because cellular processes as well as the muscles, including the heart, need potassium, and liver damage.[2]

Animals poisoned by yew first become very agitated, and subsequently their breathing becomes increasingly slow and shallow; they dribble and suffer cramps, their breathing apparatus fails and they collapse. Horses undergo increased urination, colic and paralysis, and can be dead within half an hour (sometimes within only minutes).[3] Indeed, among domesticated animals horses are the most sensitive to yew toxins. Yew leaves have the highest taxine counts in winter (taxine content in the needles differs from tree to tree, but is about 0.4 per cent in summer and about 2 per cent in winter).[4] Throughout history, horses and cattle have died after ingesting yew foliage, particularly when let into winter fields with no other green food present, or when given access to cut branches. Yew foliage can be even more poisonous when wilted or dried,[5] yet it was a traditional part of animal fodder in many regions all over Europe and the Caucasus until the introduction of artificial fodder supplements in the twentieth century. This practice still persists in some regions, for example in Albania.[6] The key is habitual access to small quantities at a time, which builds up an immunity.[7] It is a sudden excess that is fatal. Wild animals like deer and rabbits instinctively know when to stop eating the foliage. Horses do not, and are put in danger when humans cut yew hedges along their field and leave the branches accessible to the animals.

For horses and pigs, 100–200 g (3½–7 oz) of yew leaves are considered fatal; the figures are 100–250 g (3½–9 oz) for sheep and 500 g (18 oz) for cattle.[8] Goats, cats and guinea pigs are less susceptible. Between 50 and 100 g (2–3½ oz) of yew leaves can be fatal to adult humans, less for children. However, about 800 needles would be needed to provide even the minimum amount, 9 g (¼ oz), considered to be harmful to a small child.[9] There is therefore no need at all to remove yew trees from the edges of playgrounds or from parks. The red arils are obviously more attractive than the leaves, but they are not poisonous. The seeds within the arils contain taxines, but only in small amounts: to be affected, a child would have to eat 65–100 of the hard and very bitter-tasting seeds, and actually chew them thoroughly.[10] If accidentally swallowed, a seed will in all probability pass through the digestive tract whole, as do cherry stones.

The toxicity of *Taxus* has been known since prehistory, and the first written reference was recorded by the Greek scholar Theophrastus (371–287 BC).[11] Strabo (*c.* 63 BC–*c.* AD 23) and Plutarch (AD 46–after 119) said that the Gauls (Celtic tribes in France) used yew to poison their arrows.[12] Some Roman writers mused that their word for the tree, *taxus*, was not only derived from *tóxon*, the Greek for bow, but also might have been related to Greek *toxikon*, 'arrow poison'. Thus Pliny the Elder (AD 23–79) states:

> There are authors, also, who assert that the poisons which we call at the present day *toxica*, and in which arrows are dipped, were formerly called *taxica*, from this tree.[13]

However, no evidence regarding the extraction of yew toxins for the poisoning of arrowheads has ever been found.

In his classical work on medicine, the Greek physician and pharmacologist Dioscorides (AD 40–*c.* 90) stated that:

the yew growing in Narvonia [Spain] has such a power that those who sit or sleep under its shade suffer harm or in many cases may even die![14]

Was he hopelessly exaggerating (not quite his style) or is this a hint about a local genotype especially rich in taxines, a type of yew that has long been extinct? Another aspect of the taxines relates to the fact that many alkaloids have psychoactive effects – mescaline, caffeine, nicotine, morphine and cocaine, for example, all belong to the alkaloids. Indeed, some reports of altered states of consciousness relating to yew exist, and the cause was not even an oral intake of yew material, but simply breathing the air beneath big trees. In 1970, Dr A. Kukowka, a retired medical professor, was gardening beneath the branches of four yew trees for about two hours when he was overcome by dizziness, nausea, headache and disorientation. He lost his sense of time and began to hallucinate: scenes of vampires and vipers were soon followed by visions of a paradisiacal realm, heavenly music of the spheres and euphoric happiness.[15] Others have reported 'funny things' happening to them underneath certain yew trees. It seems possible that a chemical diffusion from the leaves in certain weather conditions (hot and dry, no wind) might occur. Perhaps, then, there is a core of truth to Dioscorides' statement about airborne emanations from yew.

As the great Rennaissance physician Paracelsus (1493–1541) says: *dosis sola fecit venenum*, 'the dose makes the poison'. Yew extracts have been used traditionally in herbal medicine all around the world. In the Himalayas, Nepalese medicine uses the leaves for coughs, bronchitis and asthma, and in northern India, yew preparations are employed for loosening mucus, relieving cramps, and stomach and heart problems. At least in India, yew preparations are still sold. Villagers in Afghanistan, Pakistan, Nepal, northern India, Tibet, western China and Southeast Asia, by the way, eat the arils without medicinal necessity.[16] In the Atlantic coastal regions of

North America, the Iroquois use a compound to help with menstruation, rheumatism, coughs and colds, and at times include it 'in all medicines to give them strength'. In the traditional medicine of other native cultures, yew occurs as a remedy for rheumatism, colds and gonorrhea, and as a diuretic. Women use it for irregular menses or for afterbirth pain and blood clots. On the other side of the continent, yew has a wide range of internal and external medical uses, for example for stomach pains or general internal ailments, as a dermatological poultice to put on wounds, as a wash to improve general health and as a preparation of the bark to 'purify the blood'.[17] In Europe, too, yew has been used throughout the history of allopathic medicine. In the Greco-Roman world, yew poison was used as an antidote to adder bites, to stimulate menstruation, and to treat insect bites and intestinal worms. In the old Coptic medicine of Egypt, a tea of yew leaves was used for skin problems and particularly for persistent skin ulcers. From the Middle Ages on, yew preparations were used for wounds, parasites, epilepsy, diphtheria, rheumatism, arthritis and tonsillitis. Tragically, overdosing with yew preparations frequently led to patients' deaths, particularly in desperate abortion attempts. Furthermore, yew smoke was widely used to treat rashes and scabies, as well as to expel parasites from dogs and from stables, and rodents or ghosts from the house.[18]

A completely different kind of poison in yew are the taxanes, which are not soluble in water and therefore cannot be absorbed in the digestive tract, so that they do not contribute to animal poisoning. They are, however, highly sought after for their tumour-active properties in cancer chemotherapy.

In 1958, the National Cancer Institute of the United States started a gigantic screening programme aimed at finding anti-tumour substances in nature. About 35,000 species were screened, but only one compound was found: discovered in May 1964, the tumour-active compound in yew bark was first isolated in 1966. It was named taxol, and today is called paclitaxel. After extensive chemical and clinical trials, the compound finally achieved the required official approval as a marketable drug for human cancer chemotherapy in the USA in 1992, followed by many other countries. However, because vast yew populations were destroyed by bark-stripping, the semi-synthesis of paclitaxel from the leaves rather than the bark was developed during the early 1990s, using the precursor molecule, DAB-III (short for 10-deacetylbaccatine III), and transforming it in a few steps into a semi-synthetic compound even more active than paclitaxel itself. The result, docetaxel (and the drug containing it, Taxotere®), was approved in the USA and European Union in 1996. In the UK, both products, Taxotere® and Taxol®, received their licence for the treatment of early breast cancer from the MHRA (Medicines and Healthcare Products Regulatory Authority) in January and February 2005, respectively. Taxotere® (docetaxel) for prostate cancer was approved in November 2004.

Taxanes have revolutionized the treatment options for patients with advanced forms of breast and ovarian cancers and some types of leukaemia (non small-cell lung cancer). The response rates in patients are very high. Taxanes have a chemical mechanism of action that is different from that of any other class of anti-cancer drug: they bind to the microtubules in the cancer cells. By stabilizing the microtubules, mitosis and therefore tumour growth is inhibited. It is noteworthy that the well-known terrible side effects of chemotherapy (such as hair loss, numbness, tingling or burning sensations, joint and muscle pains, anaemia and proneness to bacterial infections) for the greatest part are not caused by the yew compound itself, but by the synthetic solvent that is necessary in order to facilitate the interaction of taxane with the human body. Paclitaxel itself is a white to off-white crystalline powder that would not engage with the human metabolism because it is not soluble in water or oil. This is a general problem with all taxanes in medicine. Hence, in the pharmaceutical product Taxol®, the taxane is dissolved in polyethylated castor oil (Cremophor EL) plus ethanol. The latest research is exploring how to facilitate albumin-bound nanoparticles of paclitaxel, in order to avoid the solvents that are so detrimental to health.[19]

seven

Political Yew

🎋

The history of hunting weapons goes well back into pre-history. The oldest spears of yew wood, as well as the oldest yew bows, have been found in Europe (Denmark, Germany, Switzerland and Britain). The bows are all longbows, ranging from about 155.5 to 175 cm (5 ft 1 in to 5 ft 9 in) in length.[1] The invention of the bow was a huge advantage for humankind: it enabled the hunting of game with success and comparative safety. In areas where bow timber (the best is yew, followed by wych elm) was not readily available, such as the polar region north of the tree-line, humans developed composite bows of horn, bone, sinew and gut in various combinations. Advanced composite bows make use of the fact that horn compresses (and hence was used on the belly side that faces the archer), and that sinew is elastic and lengthens (and hence is glued on the back, the surface away from the archer). In the most developed composite bows, the speed of the limbs' return to their normal position, and thus the force of the arrow, is greater than that of any kind of timber (this is also why contemporary archery has abandoned wooden bows for composite ones). For millennia, the two superior types of bow were the short composite bow and the yew longbow, due to its sheer size and the elasticity of yew wood.

A turning point in history occurred sometime during the first three centuries of the Christian era, when Scandinavian bowyers discovered the different properties of yew sapwood and heartwood.

The heartwood compresses well (on the side facing the archer) and the sapwood (forming a thin layer on the back of the bow) is elastic and lengthens. These unique properties of yew wood make for a natural 'composite' yew bow, if the bow stave is taken from the tree where the two types of wood meet underneath the outer bark. The next stage was to combine this knowledge with the size of the longbow, creating the most effective killing device known to mankind at that time. The Neolithic hunting longbows had draw weights ranging from about 15 kg to a maximum of about 30 kg (33–66 lb). Although this gave them a maximum range of about 50 m (167 ft), a large mammal such as a deer would have needed to be as close as 5–10 m (16–32 ft) away in order to be felled.

The eighth-century Viking 'composite yew longbows' have draw weights of up to about 50 kg (110 lb), so they were not designed for hunting but for combat.[2] Weapons always seem to become ever more powerful, and by the late Middle Ages the great war bows were even heavier: their draw weights reached up to 80 kg (175 lb), with the majority reaching 63–8 kg (140–50 lb).[3] Arrows from such bows could reach about 300 m (984 ft), and could certainly still do damage at about 240 m (787 ft). At this distance the loss of velocity was only some 16 per cent. At point-blank range, almost no metal could withstand the armour-piercing tips of these arrows. In the late thirteenth century, the Gwent archers (South Wales) were feared for their ability to nail armed enemies to their saddles by piercing the armour, leg and leather saddle, and penetrating deep into the horse with a single shot. Archery became a crucial part of warfare.

Soon after Wales was subdued by the (Norman) English monarchy, King Edward I (r. 1274–1307) began to gradually incorporate archery into the English army. He decreed by law that every able-bodied man in the country, with the exception only of priests and judges, was obliged to have in his possession a bow and arrows, and to practise with them and keep them in good order, ready for immediate service.[4] The widespread use of the bow and arrow ensured

The Battle of Poitiers, 1356.

that the archery ranks could always be filled without delays – because for the next three centuries, the English army would keep a constant contingent of 5,000 or more professional archers, even in times of peace. However, does peace ever last when superior weapons are available? From the end of the thirteenth century, six infamous yew longbow battles helped to forge the Empire.

At Falkirk in 1298, Edward I defeated William Wallace's Scots. This battle is generally seen as the first classic victory for the longbow. At Bannockburn in 1314, Robert the Bruce defeated an English army twice the size of the Scottish army, partly because he found a way to ride down the inefficiently deployed and unprotected archers of the English. This was a defeat for the English, but it was also the final strategic lesson for a nation that was to take archery to its military peak. After Bannockburn, the tables turned. At Dupplin Muir in 1332, only 500 English knights and men-at-arms and about 1,500 archers defeated a Scottish army perhaps 10,000 strong.[5]

Master of the Holy Kinship (II): Altarpiece of St Sebastian, c. 1493–4, oil and gold on oakboard.

The power of the longbow then turned south and shaped the Hundred Years War (1337–1453) against France. The first decisive battle took place at Crècy in 1346, where the English were out-numbered ten to one, but still won the day: 7,000 English archers darkened the sky with 70,000 arrows per minute, 'flying in the air as thick as snow, with a terrible noise, much like a tempestuous wind preceding the tempest', an eyewitness chronicler recorded.[6] Again, at Poitiers in 1356, thousands of Frenchmen perished in an English arrow storm. However, the most cataclysmic event for France was yet to come: on Friday, 25 October 1415, near Agincourt in north-ern France, 20,000–30,000 Frenchmen, many of them mounted knights in heavy armour, were defeated by only 900 men-at-arms and 5,000 archers.[7]

England became a major political player in Western Europe – but there was a price to be paid for this. All over England and Wales, bowyers, fletchers, longbow stringmakers and arrowsmiths had to be paid, as did manufacturers of lances, swords and armour, and the producers and organizers of essential supplies to keep thousands of men alive and on the move. Archers were especially expensive because they had to keep practising all year round. In the 1270s, a yew longbow from the branch cost a shilling, and one from the bole (trunk) 1s 6d. The standard equipment of a bow, a replacement bow, 48 arrows, a quiver and a quiver belt would have cost about 5s 6d per archer; the supply of 5,000 archers therefore amounted to about £1,375 sterling. About 200 years later, in 1473, the House of Commons granted the king £51,117 4s 7d in full payment of the wages of 14,000 archers for one year. All this implied severe taxation of every town, city and county. There were additional demands: for example, in February 1417, six feathers from every goose in twenty southern counties had to be at the Tower by the following March, and documents for the following year state that the sheriffs had to supply 1,190,000 goose feathers for distribution to the workshops of the arrowsmiths.[8]

> *England would be but a fling*
> *If not for the yew and the grey goose wing.*
> OLD BRITISH PROVERB

Where did all the yew staves come from? Yew was certainly *not* grown in churchyards to supply the army. In fact, the entire British Isles was far too small to satisfy the military hunger for yew wood. Edward II (r. 1307–27) had to import yew staves from Ireland and Spain (one record mentions a cargo of 180 dozen Spanish bows for £36),[9] yet in around 1350, demand began to seriously outstrip supply. What happened next has been 'forgotten' in British history for over 700 years: an international trade in yew timber developed, with shipments from Baltic, German, Dutch, Spanish, French and Italian harbours reaching English seaports, mainly London. An unprecedented hunt for a single species of tree began, which lasted for four centuries.[10] The centre of attention was the Alpine regions with their extensive mixed forests, but large numbers of yew staves also came from the far off Carpathian Mountains in Eastern Europe and the Mediterranean forests in Spain, Italy and Albania. The continental wood was superior to that of British yews because for the most part it derived from slow growth at higher altitudes, compared with the more favourable growth conditions in wet lowland Britain.

This vast trade network is well documented in manuscripts from a range of continental countries. The oldest document relating to the trade of bow timber is a customs scroll from the Dutch city of Dordrecht, dated 10 October 1287, while the first evidence of an actual import of bow timber into England dates from 1294. On 8 January 1295, six ships from Stralsund in the Baltic Sea brought 360 *baculi ad arcus* (bow staves) to Newcastle, but the principle city for yew imports was London, which even hosted an entire bowyers' quarter. For a long time this set-up of imported yew timber remained unsatisfactory because the English kings had to set price limits for bows so that all 'able-bodied men' in the country could afford to take part in the compulsory archery training. The controlled bow prices were too low to serve as an efficient incentive for importers – after all, they had to cover the high costs of obtaining and transporting the raw bow staves across Europe. This problem was only solved by the Statute of Westminster of 1472, which decreed 'that for every tun-tight of merchandise . . . four bowestaffes be brought' by ships and vessels unloading in any English harbour. This law ingeniously shifted the yew supply pressure from the government to the trading companies. The compulsory import of yew staves, enforced by the threat of heavy penalties, led to an early capitalistic monopoly in the central European forestry and timber trade – and the annihilation of the majority of Europe's yew stands.

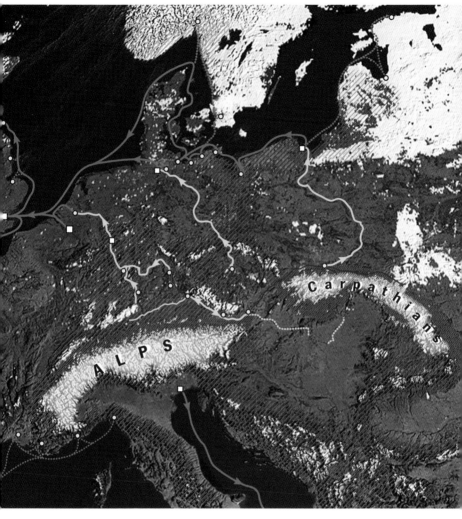

By the early 16th century, the network of yew stave transport routes extended all over Europe.

On the other side of the Channel, regional governments and monarchs wanted their share of the vibrant yew trade. In Bavaria, Tyrol, and Upper and Lower Austria, the trading companies had to petition the royal authorities and put in bids for a so-called *Eibenmonopol*, the Yew Monopoly or Privileges, for a certain area. An *Eibenmonopol* guaranteed exclusive rights for the extraction of yew timber from a defined

A Yew Monopoly, signed by Albrecht, duke of Bavaria, in 1551.

area for a number of years (usually three to six) to these private trading companies. The only obligations for the trading company were: it had to spare other trees and also yew trees that were too young; the woodcutters had to be experienced in bow stave-cutting (a wrong cut can waste everything) and were to be monitored; and the sale of yew staves to the 'infidels', the Tartars and Turks in the East, was absolutely forbidden. Most importantly, a Yew Privilege regulated the export volume (usually 20,000 staves per year), the payment of tolls, customs and forest tax and, last but not least, the sum to be paid to the royal treasury. For example, in 1521 the Austrian monarchy demanded 5 Rhineland guilders per thousand bow staves for the Yew Privilege for Tyrol, and Balthasar Lurtsch bought a volume of 20,000 staves. He was outbid two years later by the company of Joachim Rehle, which offered the unrealistic amount of 100 Rhineland guilders, but he did not pay in the end, and five years later the fluctuating rate finally settled again, at 32 guilders per 1,000 staves. The astronomical proportions of the yew trade can be understood by looking at the company of Christoph Fürer & Leonard Stockhammer, for which documents spanning 80 years (1512–1592) have survived. During this period, this company alone exported 1.6 million yew staves – and there were many other companies.

The ecological disaster did not happen overnight. A number of documents, particularly from the Alpine countries, reveal the grow-ing concern and even resistance to the wholesale destruction of yew stands. The first negotiations for a total ban on felling yew wood in both Bavaria and Austria appear as early as 1507 – just 35 years after Edward IV had first decreed compulsory yew imports. Just like today, calls for the protection of the forests remained largely unheeded for too long. In 1518, some measures against illegal felling were taken, and a ten-year felling cessation was agreed (far too short), but otherwise business went on as usual. Fourteen years later, in 1532, an ominous comment upon the volume of exports appeared in Bavarian docu-ments: the usual number of yew staves was granted 'if there are that many'. In 1542, the Bavarian government wrote a letter to the deputy of the Holy Roman Emperor, Charles V, which was an intense plea to leave the yews alone. This document sheds some light on the felling practices of the time, indicating that it was not only young or cop-piced yews that were being felled for bows (a 100-year-old yew yields just four bow staves). All sizes and ages were being felled, even includ-ing old or ancient trees whose fall left critical gaps in the forest where 'wind breaks occur immediately, which brings great damage and dis-advantage to the high and low conifer forests and also the home forests of the subjects [of your majesty]'.[11] The letter also mentions

An old yew in Bavaria, one of the few survivors of the 'longbow mania'.

how much wood is wasted and left behind because only the area where heartwood and sapwood meet is used for bows, and states that yews have been severely depleted, and that only young trees and brushwood are left. However, it could not prevent the continuation of the monopoly practice. The year 1589 finally marked the total end of the granting of Yew Privileges for Bavaria as well as Austria because no trees of any worthwhile size were left.

Some of the English kings had tried to be helpful: Richard III ordered a general planting of yew in 1483, and in 1511 Henry VIII (r. 1509–47), while reinforcing the compulsory imports, decreed the planting of yews everywhere in England.[12] Such measures were far from adequate. The collapse came during the reign of Queen Elizabeth I (r. 1558–1603). In response to the crisis, her Act of Bowyers decreed that for every bow of yew, a bowyer had to produce four of inferior wood, for example wych elm. By then, yew had become so scarce that yew bows had to be shared around, and those under seventeen were forbidden to shoot 'in a yew bow'. With the supplies from Central Europe running dry, Elizabeth also enforced yew stave imports from the Hanse towns by the Baltic Sea (Carpathian yews coming via Poland). It was all in vain: on 26 October 1595, Elizabeth I decreed that the army was to replace its longbows with shotguns.[13] At this time all firearms were still far inferior to the longbow, and would remain so for another 200 years. A longbow could outshoot a musket with six arrows launched for every bullet fired, with greater reach and precision. There was, however, no other choice to be made – the trees had gone.

Right across Europe yew populations were exhausted, and until today they have never recovered. The post-medieval spread of farming and livestock breeding, and the change in forestry from mixed coppice to broadleaved timber production, did not give *Taxus* a chance to regain the regions it once graced. Today, Germany, Austria and Switzerland together have less than ten ancient yews left, France, Spain and Italy have somewhat higher counts, but Britain, thanks to graveyards and remote cliff populations, has about 1,300 ancient and veteran yews. In all countries except Britain, the survivors of the 'longbow mania' are protected by law. Botanists and foresters around the globe are looking at Britain, wondering if it will finally begin to acknowledge the treasure it holds: its moral debt as well as the unfathomable scientific value (genetically, for example) of the oldest living things in Europe.

eight
Aesthetic Yew
✺

With the coming of the Renaissance, which started in early fifteenth-century Italy, there began a comparatively peaceful and prosperous time for European societies. Italian city-states started to thrive, and all over Europe private tradespeople began to accumulate riches. Castles were changed from fortified strongholds to shining palaces surrounded by large gardens that served the purposes of pleasure and representing status. Elaborate garden and landscape design became an expression of a new vision of art and culture. Italy remained the cradle and school of European garden art for about 200 years, but in the mid-sixteenth century, France adapted Italian garden design and developed the French or Baroque garden, with its typical large-scale ground plan and its profusion of geometric and animal shapes ranging from the stunning to the ridiculous. The 'art' of clipping yew trees and hedges into almost any desired shape made *Taxus baccata* a key element in French gardening, above all other evergreens. The present head gardener at the Château de Versailles, Alain Baraton, commented in 2010 on the psychology behind the clipped yews in French gardening:

> from the seventeenth century, man felt the need to make his mark on nature. He felt the need to control nature. Tame it. And there was nothing as simple as trimming a yew into any shape one wanted. . . . This also gave the king . . . the

French formal garden, Château de Villandry, Loire Valley.

French topiary in the palace gardens at Versailles.

opportunity to show his subjects that he not only commanded men – he also commanded nature![1]

We might add that he commanded not only nature, but also the
English yew.

The French garden style with its topiary fell out of international fashion again in around 1760. It was replaced by the 'English
garden' with its return to natural forms.[2] A key figure in this horticultural transition was William Robinson (1838–1935), who is regarded
by many as the inventor of gardening as we know it today. Robinson
loathed Versailles as 'indescribable ugliness and emptiness',[3] and
campaigned for informal planting and the qualities of native plants.
He devised his ideas beneath two handsome (unclipped) yew trees
in his garden at Gravetye Manor in West Sussex. The trees are still
there.[4] Today, over 100 garden varieties of yew are offered by garden
centres, far more than of any other conifer. The most famous and
characteristic variety of yew is the Irish yew (*Taxus baccata* var. *fasti-
giata*). First discovered in the 1760s on a rock (Carricknamaddow)
in the hills near Florence Court, Co. Fermanagh, cuttings were given

French topiary near the Hagia Sophia in Istanbul, Turkey.

a few decades later to English nurseries, which propagated and distributed them. All Irish yews are descended from the parent plant at Florence Court because, like the other garden varieties, they do not breed true but revert to the original form of *Taxus baccata*.[5]

The beauty of the wood of yew has been recognized since early times: yew veneer was known in ancient Egypt, where yew was a rare and precious wood used for grave furniture and sarcophagi in the tombs of the Sixth, Eleventh and Twelfth Dynasties, and in the Eighteenth Dynasty (*c.* 1355 BC) for two busts of Queen Teye.[6] The Hellenistic Greeks, according to Theophrastus, used it for armchairs, chests and other furniture. In Athens, archaeologists unearthed a yew comb and bedpost from the Archaic period (*c.* 700–*c.* 500 BC). In early Greece, yew was also one of the principal woods, along with cypress, juniper and oak, for carving images of the gods.[7] Further east, yew wood was used in the construction of the royal tomb at Gordion (the capital of the ancient kingdom of Phrygia, now modern eastern Turkey), which is also called Midas Mound, after the legendary king whose touch turned everything into gold. The mausoleum is about 2,600 years old, and inside the chamber were two

Irish yew, stamp from Ireland, 1984.

Spice cupboard, 17th century, England.

Child's mask for Noh theatre, late 20th century, Japan.

wooden screens measuring 195 x 80 cm (76 x 31 in) decorated with intricate inlay work made of dark yew wood, providing a striking contrast to the white boxwood into which they were fitted.[8]

Another area where yew outcompetes other timbers is music. With its tight grain, yew wood provides excellent sound transmission and makes fabulous musical instruments. The oldest known wooden instruments in the world are the yew pipes at Greystones, Ireland, which are about 4,100 years old. They were not a part of a bagpipe but, rather surprisingly, an element of a kind of small organ. Wood does not preserve well so early wooden instruments are extremely rare, but other very old artefacts comprise the four curved pipes from Killyfadda, Co. Tyrone (400 BC), the Bekan Horn from Co. Mayo and a short, conical wooden horn from the River Erne in Co. Fermanagh (both AD 700). All these were preserved in the damp soils of Ireland, which are favourable to wood preservation.[9] Historical examples include lutes from fifteenth- and sixteenth-century Bavaria. For the round backs of the sound bodies of these lutes (forerunners

Hans Diebschlag, *The Ancient Yew at Barlavington*, 2008, watercolour on paper.

of the guitar), their masterful makers steam bent strips of yew wood about 50 cm (20 in) long into semicircular form and laminated them together. Yew wood is the only coniferous wood that does not crack in steam bending.[10] This craft perished with the destruction of the continental yew populations caused by the longbow trade. Other historical examples of musical instruments include eighteenth-century flutes and bassoons (solid yew), and two Viennese fortepianos (yew veneer) from the early nineteenth century.

The Renaissance and Baroque periods saw furniture making reach new and unprecedented heights, and the decorative value of yew was in very high demand. This remained the case during the seventeenth century for fashionable grandfather-clock cases with yew veneer and gateleg tables in particular, and during the eighteenth century for chair making in the Windsor style. Yew wood became even more popular during the Victorian era, for all kinds of fine furniture.[11] Some demand could be satisfied with young yew trees that had been growing since the longbow catastrophe, but imports were probably always welcome. In the nineteenth century, Georgia finally strayed from the yew protection decreed by Queen Tamara in the early thirteenth century and raided its yew populations almost entirely for export to shipbuilders in Turkey, Greece and Italy.[12]

More sustainable ways of appreciating the beauty of a tree are through poetry and fine art. There is not much to report about yew in painting; the tree largely vanished from the face of Europe. Painters also did not feel attracted to graveyards, where yew trees did grow – unlike poets, it seems.

Yew appears in Western poetry from the seventeenth century onwards, but nothing is ever really said about the tree as it is. All texts merely reflect the image of the tree at the time: a harbinger of tragedy and death, living on dead men's flesh, at best providing a dark mood to a poem, at worst accused of being the haunt of ghosts, demons or the devil himself. John Webster (1580–1625) moralizes in *The White Devil* 'Like the black and melancholy Yew Tree, Dost think to root thyself in dead men's graves, And yet to prosper?', and Abraham Cowley (1618–1667) speaks of 'black Yew's unlucky green' (*The Complaint*).[13] By comparison, William Shakespeare's treatment had been mild: in accord with the folklore of his time, he lets Macbeth's witches stir 'Gall of goat, and slips of yew Sliver'd in the Moon's eclipse' into their boiling cauldron (IV. i. 28–9). In all fairness, Shakespeare was also one of the first writers who did break the mould. He alludes to the deeper layers of the yew's potential when in *Romeo and Juliet* the tree stimulates a dream of the future: 'As I did sleep under this yew tree here, I dreamt my master and another fought, And that my master slew him' (V, iii, 3–7). However, in the seventeenth and eighteenth centuries (and no earlier), yew became known as the 'tree of death'. The reasons for this are plain: the tree was seen mostly in graveyards, and associated only with the mass longbow slaughters of the Middle Ages. This twisted image of the tree lasted well into our times, and also had a profound effect on the interpretation of the mythical northern World Tree as an ash.

The first poets to overcome the conventional doom and gloom cliché of *Taxus* and ascend to new visions of transformation and transcendence are to be found among the Romantics. William Words-worth (1770–1850), who introduced a new perception of nature in the late eighteenth century, was the first to suggest the redemptive possibilities of the natural world. He wrote a monumental poem in praise of the 'fraternal Four', the ancient yews at Borrowdale, and the solitary yew at Lorton (Cumbria), 'a living thing Produced too slow-ly ever to decay; Of form and aspect too magnificent to be destroyed'.[14] However, only with T. S. Eliot (1888–1965) did yew again become what it once had been in prehistoric times: the symbol not of death but of immortality. In 'Ash Wednesday', written in 1930, Eliot depicts a mysterious female in the yew's vicinity. As if transported to another, timeless dimension, the poet glimpses her as a veiled 'sister', and the world stands still until the wind shakes 'a thousand whispers from the yew'. Returning to our world, he henceforth feels in 'exile'.[15] The influential German poet Annette von Droste-Hülshoff (1797–1848) similarly indicates a strong personal experience of an expanded consciousness when she says:

> They say, that sleep, a bad one
> Exudes from your needles –
> Alas! Never was I more awake
> Than being surrounded by you.[16]

How many writers may have received inspiration beneath yew trees but never talked about it? We will never know, but among those whose works pioneered some entirely new grounds are many who had almost certainly visited impressive ancient yews such as those found in Druids Grove in Surrey, southern England: E. M. Forster (*A Passage to India*), Thomas Hardy (*Tess of the d'Urbervilles*), Sir James Barrie (*Peter Pan*), Lewis Carroll (*Alice's Adventures in Wonderland*), the poets A. C. Swinburne and W. B. Yeats, and the young G. M. Trevelyan.[17] R. L. Stevenson (1850–1894, *Treasure Island*) used to play in an old yew tree that today still shows the remains of his swing hanging from one of its branches. Now known as Stevenson's Yew, the tree has a girth of 3.64 m (12 ft) and is a living link with one of Scotland's great literary figures. Stevenson loved it all his life: 'A yew, which is one of the glories of the village . . .'.[18] Another garden yew, this one in Berlin in 1826, acted as a muse for the young composer Felix Mendelssohn-Bartholdy (1809–1847) who, at the tender age of seventeen, composed the music for a production of Shakespeare's *A Midsummer Night's Dream*. 'Under the tree's canopy interwoven with sparkling moonlight', Mendelssohn 'heard the music of dancing elves therein' – so much so that he insisted that the premiere of *A Midsummer Night's Dream* should take place under the very yew itself.[19]

After moving to the small village of Downe, Kent, in southern England in 1842, the English naturalist Charles Darwin (1809–1882) grew to enjoy the solitude of Downe's ancient churchyard yew (girth

The Borrowdale Yews, painting from 1905.

9.22 m/30 ft in 1999), beneath which he often sat while taking a break on his daily walk. Later, he wished to be buried beneath the old yew tree, and indeed, the day after his death on 19 April 1882, the local papers announced that he would be buried in St Mary's church-yard at Downe. Although 'Darwin had expected to be placed here',[20] influential groups had other ideas and succeeded with their plans for a state burial: the canon of Westminster Abbey was persuaded to bury the agnostic, and Darwin was accorded the ultimate British accolade of burial in Westminster Abbey, London, on 26 April 1882. Other historical figures did get their wish to be buried beneath a yew, T. S. Eliot and Lewis Carroll (Charles Dodgson),[21] for example. William Wordsworth even planted eight yew trees himself in the churchyard of St Oswald's, Grasmere, Cumbria, and later he and his wife Mary were buried beneath one of them.

Times kept changing. The massive cultural changes of the nineteenth century – industrialization, rationalism and physical materialism – also triggered an opposite philosophy: an emphasis on the individual, the imaginative, the emotional, the visionary and even the transcendental. Romanticism and its deepened appreci-ation of the beauties of nature had been leaving its mark since the late eighteenth century. All of this fused into the spirit of the nine-teenth century and a changing attitude towards nature and the 'envi-ronment'. In 1819, the German naturalist and explorer Alexander von Humboldt (1769–1859) coined the term 'tree monument' for the pro-tection of ancient trees.[22] Six years later the first suggestions for the protection of nature began to appear in literature, and in 1860 the first negotiations regarding the conservation of natural areas, and also of birds, were under way. In 1906 in Western Prussia (modern Poland), after working in yew conservation for a quarter of a centu-ry, Hugo Conwentz became the director of Europe's first 'national office for the conservation of natural monuments'.[23]

With this context in mind we may not be surprised at a few sudden 'outbreaks' of sheer yew sympathy occurring in northwest-ern Europe. Faced with the problem that a certain tree was in the way

Bettws-y-coed Old Church and Yew Tree.

Mid-20th-century postcard from North Wales.

of development and threatened with loss of life, it was suggested that the tree should be *moved* instead of being felled. Unheard of before, this task was performed in the churchyard of Buckland-in-Dover in the early spring of 1880. To make space for a new church extension, the tree needed to be moved 18 m (60 ft). A huge block of earth around its roots, measuring 5.4 x 4.8 m (18 x 16 ft), was cut out, a trench leading to the new location was dug, and with the help of huge planks of timber, chains, rollers and windlasses 'the whole mass of the tree, estimated at 55 tons, began to move'.[24] The whole operation took nine days. The tree lives today and there is no reason why it should not live for many more centuries. The idea itself, however, was not entirely new.

The possibility of moving a tree had already been discussed in Berlin in the 1850s, when the Prussian king, Frederick William IV, wanted to save a yew tree he had known from childhood from an extension to the building where the Government's Upper House met. Because of the lack of experience in tree removal, the yew was left where it was and instead the king had the building plans changed, so that the new walls stopped short of the tree.[25] The most spectacular tree relocation occurred in 1907 in Frankfurt, Germany. When the

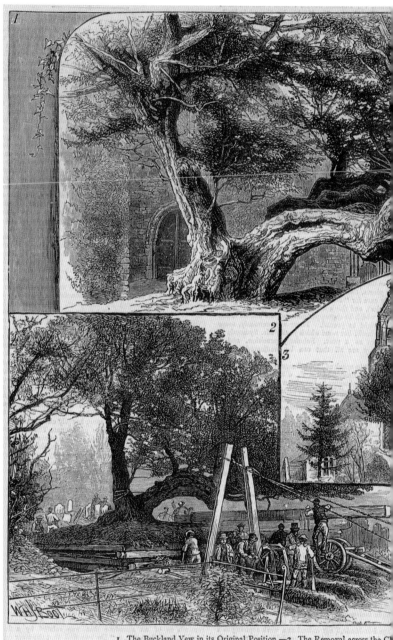

1. The Buckland Yew in its Original Position.—2. The Removal across the Ch

TRANSPLANTATION OF THE ANCIENT "B

ree after Transplantation.

YEW" AT DOVER

Yew transplantation at Buckland-in-
Dover, illustration from 1880.

'The arrival and festive reception of the yew tree': information poster from the Frankfurt tree transplantation.

Die Ankunft und der festliche Empfang
des Eibenbaums

nach seiner 25 tägigen Fahrt durch Frankfurt a. M. an seinem
neuen Standort im Botanischen Garten, neben dem Palmengarten,
am Eingang der Miquelstrasse.

Botanical Garden had to be moved from the centre of the expanding city to a new location 3.5 km (2.2 miles) away, a total of 4,340 plants were moved, but only one tree: a yew with a 73 cm (29 in) trunk diameter, a height of 12 m (39 ft) and an estimated age of 230 to 260 years. This time, advice was at hand, and in 1905 a consultant from England was brought in. Following his advice, the block of earth and the roots were tentatively cut almost two years before the removal, so that the tree could develop a denser network of fine roots close to the centre. In this way, the block of earth could be limited to a square of 4 m (13 ft) at a depth of 2 m (6½ ft). The block of earth was framed in a wooden box, and the whole 42.5 tons were moved on a system of rollers and pulled by two steam-rollers. In order to protect the roads from collapsing under this enormous weight and plummeting into the sewers beneath, a cross-hatching of wooden planks was laid out in front of the tree to distribute the weight more evenly across a wider surface. Overhead tram

Frankfurt tree transplantation, postcard from 1907.

wires had to be removed in places. The moving of the yew tree was an extremely popular event, and the entire journey of seventeen days was accompanied by crowds of people.[26] This tree is still thriving today.

nine

Metaphysical Yew

꽃

The first point of call in the examination of the older strata of the cultural history of a tree is language. Names reveal a lot – and also hide a lot. Nowadays, the most common globally used name for yew is its botanical name, *Taxus*, which is also reflected in most Latin languages (Italian *tasso*, Spanish *tejo*), in Portuguese (*teixo*) and in the Slavonic languages (Russian *tiss*, Polish *cís*, Czech, Slovak *tís* and Slovenian *tisa*, for example). The probable origin of the Latin *tax-* is the Indo-European *tak*, 'to cut', which extended into *taks*, 'to hew, to shape', and also *teks*, 'to make, to manufacture'. *Tax* is related to *tag*, *tangere*, 'to touch'.[1]

The other widespread word for the tree is of course the English one. The Old English *iw, eow, eoh* (poetic), later *eugh*, Old Saxon *ioh* and Old Norse *yr* are related to the Old Prussian *iuwis* (*iwis*) and Middle High German *iwe*, and they all trace back to the Old High German *iwe, iwa*. Here we catch a glimpse of the ancient meaning of the name – this term for yew is closely related to the Old High German *ewi, ewa*, which means 'eternity'. Additionally, the Saxon dialect forms, *eo, io, eoh, eow*, stem from the Old High German *eo*, 'always'.[2] The oldest Celtic names are *eber* and *eburos* from Gaul (modern France), followed by the Old Irish *eo, íbhar, íbar, jubar*. Their original meaning can be assumed to have been similar to that of the Germanic names, as the Celtic and Germanic languages share a common ancestry in so-called Indo-European. Digging deeper, the Indo-European *ayu*, 'life force', has been suggested as a root word for both the Germanic

Morning light in a yew tree.

iwe and the Celtic *eber*. It is even apparent in the oldest name for yew
that has come down to us, the ancient Hittite *eya*.[3] Recalling the
extraordinary levels of yew's electrical currents, this ancient association with life force seems more than apt.

The past importance and significance of a tree can also be seen
in the linguistic landscape. In Europe, places named after yew abound,
for example Eborakon (York) in northeast England, Château d'If in
France; Yverdon in Switzerland; Iburg in Germany; and Eburini,
Inveruno and Invorio in Italy. The Iberian Peninsula is named after
its ancient inhabitants whom the Greeks called Iberians, after the
River Ebro (Iberus), which must have had extensive yew populations in the past. The longest river of the Peninsula, the Tajo (Spanish)
or Tejo (Portuguese), is also named after yew. So were Celtic tribes like
the Iuverni, Eburovices, Eburobrigen and Eburomagus; and the

Eburones, whose king, Catuvoleus, took his own life in 53 BC by taking yew poison to avoid the shame of Roman captivity.[4]

In the Middle Ages, Georgia in the Caucasus was known as Iberia, and the native Georgian names for the tree are *chvyturi che*, 'divine tree', *tciminda che*, 'sacred tree' and *chvaebis che*, 'Tree of God'. The Japanese name, *ichii*, means 'number one rank', a prestigious reference to the Imperial inauguration ceremony in which a new Emperor is given a yew-wood sceptre as a symbol of sovereignty. Japanese Shinto priests also use a ceremonial yew staff. In the mythological origins of Japanese culture, yew is inextricably linked with Hachiman, the divine protector of Japan and its people, and with Jimmu Tenno, Japan's legendary first Emperor and direct descendant of the sun-goddess Amaterasu. The yew sceptre indicates that a new Emperor is in harmony with the will and the ancient rites of the land. In the old language of the Ainu (the indigenous people of Hokkaido, the northernmost island of Japan), yew is called *onco*, which again means 'Tree of God'.[5]

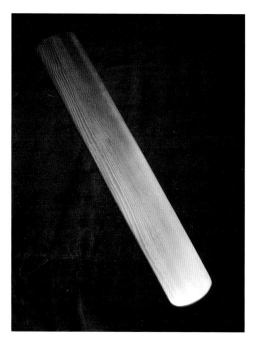

The imperial sceptre of Japan, the *shaku*, is made of yew wood.

132

Protective statue at
the Hachimanjinja
sanctuary, Japan.

The theme of the king receiving his power from the guardian
spirit of the land can be found around the globe. This ancient concept expresses the attitude of asking for permission for the changes
to the landscape that human occupation (via hunting, farming
practices, forest management and so on) inevitably asserts. The
Earth belonged to herself and not to man – a concept that today we
may call profoundly ecological.

When the Indo-European Hittites came to Anatolia in the
eighteenth century BC, they retained much of the older, indigenous
religion of the Hattians: only the goddess of the land, the 'throne-
goddess', had the power to 'adopt' a candidate for kingship and to
bestow the royal insignia. In their ceremonial pact the king agreed
to administer and protect the inhabited land as well as to respect her
territory, the wild mountains. As recorded on various cuneiform
tablets, their ritual union was sanctified by the power of the sacred

The shrine at the Hachimanjinja sanctuary. Japan.

tree: 'As the yew-tree [*eya*] is ever verdant and does not shed its leaves, even so may king and queen be thriving.'[6] Periodically re-enacted in ritual, the king, on behalf of his people, received the gifts of prosperity under the sacred tree:

> From the yew [*eya*] is suspended a hunting bag [made from the skin] of a sheep. In [the bag] lies sheep fat. In it lie [symbols of] animal fecundity and wine. In it lie [symbols of] cattle and sheep. In it lie longevity and progeny. In it lies the gentle message of the lamb . . . In it lie plenty, abundance, and satiety.[7]

To receive one had to be worthy, hence the retrieval of magical objects is a widespread motif in ancient myth and ritual. In early Greece, such competitions developed into the grand athletic games such as those of Olympia and Delphi, and found a reflection in legends like the one of Jason and the Golden Fleece.[8] Jason, too, becomes king after retrieving the symbols of fertility from the sacred tree. His initiation journey with the Argonauts takes him to a mythical land in the east, Colchis in Georgia (Iberia, 'land of yew'). He only succeeds because Medea, who is the daughter of the king, as well as a priestess of the goddess Kirke, the guardian of the world pillar, accepts him as the future king and husband. Medea also commands a magical cauldron of regeneration and the art of healing. Later, Medea and Jason hold a sacred marriage (*hieros gamos*) in the cave where Dionysos ('God's tree') was nursed.[9] The Hittite origins of the Greek 'golden fleece' legend leave no doubt that the ultimate symbol of life and renewal is the evergreen tree, and that the 'golden' token of fertility in this rite is a pollen cloud from a male yew branch rather than a dead sheepskin. Apollonius Rhodius describes the fleece in the third century BC as: a 'cloud' glowing in the sunrise; throwing a 'blush like flame' over Jason's forehead and cheeks when he picks it from the tree; and the ground beginning to sparkle brilliantly as he walks with it.[10] In an old Hittite legend, the mother-goddess Hannahanna sends out the bee to bring her the fleece, and the insect returns and puts the 'fleece' in a bowl in front of the sitting

Jason's Golden Fleece was not a dead sheepskin but a living symbol of renewal.

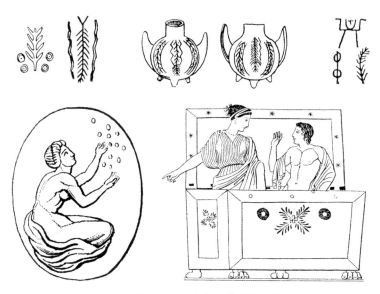

top row: Ancient yew symbols on finds from Troy.
bottom left: Danaë's pollen cloud.
bottom right: Danaë's chest decorated with yew branches and arils.

goddess.[11] The ritual significance of pollen can also be glimpsed when Zeus, 'the bright one', appears in the legend of Danaë, an earth priestess of the sea-faring Danaeans, whom he impregnates in the guise of a golden, fertilizing cloud. When she and her son, the great hero Perseus, are sent away from Argos, they travel in an ark or chest decorated with yew branches and arils. Ancient Greek sources say that Danaë travelled west, to Italy,[12] so did the worship of the Roman goddess Diana arrive in the Italian peninsula with Greek travellers? Diana is the 'goddess of the gateway tree to the underworld', like the old-Irish goddess Dana.

The similarities between southeastern and northwestern Europe are striking. In pre-Christian Ireland – which was originally called *Ierne*, later *Iverna, Iuvern(i)a* and *Hibernia*, all meaning 'yew island'[13] – kings gained the political right to rule by claiming descent from the sacred yew tree. This reverence for the tree is older than Celtic culture, but the Celtic invaders respected the ancient 'yew deities' from the very beginning. Dana (or Danu) was an ancestral mother-goddess of

Ireland, a solar deity as well as the Queen of the Underworld, and the ancestor of the first generation of gods of Ireland, the Tuatha dé Danaan. One of her epithets is Búannan, 'the lasting one'. Her mythic sons and her brother all have yew names: Eogabal, 'fork in a yew tree', Uainide, 'yew foliage' and Fer I, 'man of yew', the latter being able to create a 'yew tree of incredible beauty' out of nothing and in no time. Dana's father, the great Dagda, also bears a yew epithet: Eochu, 'mighty', derived from *ivo-katu-s*, 'who fights with yew'.[14] In Irish legends dating from about the fourth to the tenth century, the warrior elite protecting the royal house of Tara, the residence of the high king of Celtic Ireland, is called the *Craeb Ruad*, the 'Knights of the Red Branch'. Later in the Middle Ages, the composers of Arthurian legend would use this fellowship as the prototype for the Knights of the Round Table.[15]

The Germanic goddess Freyja, too, unites the celestial and terrestrial realms, and holds the power to determine the rise and fall of kings.[16] She is a goddess of love as well as of death, and originally it

The 'red branch' from Ireland.

The small 'acorn' and red 'apple' are both normal yew fruits, just in different stages of development

was she who was thought to receive the souls of the dead, to transform them to a new state of being, to rebirth (only much later, in Viking times, did the warrior aristocracy propagate the idea that the dead would go to Odin's warrior hall, Valhalla). Freyja is a deity of 'unfailing regenerative power',[17] and is also known under the name Idun (Iduna), who supplies the 'apples' of eternal youth to the gods. She can resume a 'nut shape' and regenerate herself from this seed to anthropomorphic appearance.[18] Iduna's name appears to be strongly related to the Irish Dana/Danu and also to the oriental Ida, the name of the sacred mountain in Crete, where Zeus was nursed, and of Mt Ida in Anatolia, where Zeus united with Hera, encompassed by a *golden* cloud. Both mountains called Ida had been named after their trees.[19] Idun's father is called Ivaldi, 'ruling in yew',[20] a deity generally associated with Ullr, the mythical prime archer who lives in Ydalir, 'yew valley'. In fact, the abode of all the twelve divine powers (Asgard) is located in Idavelli, also a 'yew valley'.[21]

As to Iduna's 'apples', the allusion to yew arils as apples, acorns and nuts can be found throughout history – for example, a Hittite text describes *eya* as a 'mountain-apple', and the Icelandic *Volsung saga* speaks of an 'oak' that carries 'apples'. During the 'reign' of the Tuatha de Danaan, the 'five sacred trees of Ireland' were planted from the seeds of a legendary branch with three kinds of fruit: apples, acorns and nuts. In Celtic legend, one of the five sacred trees of Ireland, Eo Mugna ('yew of Mugna'), is praised as 'blest with various virtues, with three choice fruits, The acorn, and the dark narrow nut, and the apple'.[22]

For the Hittites, yew was a cherished tree not only for kings but also for common citizens. Yew was the protector of gates: 'at whose gate the yew-tree is visible [his house is free from imposts]'. This protective spirit was called Apulunas,[23] and was present in suburban front gardens. This tradition was imported into early Greece, and in Classical times Apollo *Agyíeus* stood as a wooden pillar (it was too hot and dry for living yews in lowland cities) in front of Greek houses to ward off evil from the doors.[24] Although his name changed to Greek Apollon, he never hid his origin, as another of his epithets is *Letoídes*, 'son of Leto'. Leto is an ancient Anatolian mother-goddess associated with *eya*, the yew, and she gives birth leaning on her tree:[25] hence Apollo is born under the tree, if not *from* the tree. So is his sister Artemis, the Greek goddess of the wilderness (especially mountains), who remained connected with yew in her cult in various ways. Both Apollo and Artemis practise archery and Artemis kills her enemies with yew-poisoned arrows.

Artemis, and her darker aspect, Hekate, were venerated as divine patrons of childbirth and midwifery as well as of funeral rites. Around 300 BC, Artemis' main sanctuary in the Peloponnese, the Artemision, was located in a yew grove.[26] In Rome, black bulls sacrificed to Hekate were adorned with yew wreaths around their necks.[27] In Liguria (northern Italy), the counterpart of Artemis and of Freyja was called Diana,

clockwise from top left:
The winged goddess
Nemesis, with sacred
bough and serpent,
Greek gem made of
red jasper.

Double axe and sacred
branch, coin from Caria
(Turkey), 1st century BC.

Diana with deer and
sacred 'apple bough',
Roman gem made
of cornelian.

Apollo with tree,
hound and bow,
coin from Crete,
4th century BC.

and she also unites the themes of birth and death: she is the patroness
of birth, and as Diana *Aegeria* is the 'goddess of the gateway tree to the
underworld'. Most famous today, 'foam-born' Aphrodite is not just
the goddess of love, but started her divine career as a goddess of vegetation and Queen of the Mountain,[28] Mt Ida in Asia Minor to be exact,
where sacred marriage rites were performed. She, too, is associated
with 'apples', the underworld and furthermore the Furies (*Erinyes*),
otherworldly agents who ensured the fulfilment of the decrees of the
Fates. The Furies were imagined as fearsome wild women swaying
torches of yew wood and punishing the human breach of (divine) law
with yew poison.[29]

In the entire context of the tree's meaning, connecting burial rites
with the World Tree is almost a by-product of the celebrations of life,
as much as death is part of life. Where else should anyone want to
be buried if not beneath the Tree of Life? Yew represents the gates
between the worlds, and hence features in the burial customs of the
Celtic and Germanic tribes, and the Romans, Greeks, Phrygians,
Georgians, Saxons, Merovingians and others. Yews grace graves
in Japan, and the indigenous Tlingit people on the Pacific coast of

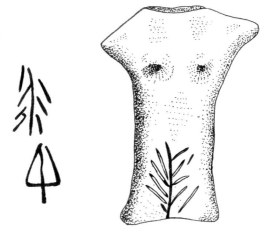

Palaeolithic (*left*) and Neolithic (*right*) birth symbolism with sacred branch.

the Alaska Peninsula have a tradition of carving death masks and spirit whistles from yew wood.[30]

The association of birth and death and of the regenerative powers of nature with the evergreen yew tree go back to prehistoric times. The above-mentioned goddesses associated with yew developed from archaic female deities of the mountains, goddesses of the land and bestowers of wisdom and inspiration whom the Greeks later called the Muses, from the Greek *Moûsa*, 'Mountain-mothers'. In Hellenistic times, there were still temples and altars to and statues of the Muses all over the Greek world.[31] All that is left now is our word *museum* – ironically, because one of the social and political functions of this aspect of mythology is to teach humans something about ecological balance and living in harmony with the land.

The metaphysical character of yew is taking shape now: a *living* symbol of eternity, a maker of kings, a Tree of God, the guardian of the gates of both death and birth, the cauldron of regeneration and rebirth, the world pillar, protector of divine law, bestower of wisdom and inspiration. Spiritually, this list is indeed of 'first rank' (*ichii*) and nothing short of the ancient universal concept of the World Tree.

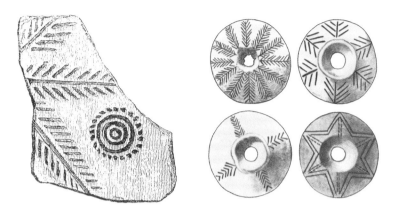

Symbology of the World Tree and the 'sacred centre': terracotta fragment, Troy I, c. 3000–2300 BC (*left*) and votive spindles, terracotta, Troy IV, c. 2100–1900 BC (*right*).

The World Tree connects our world with the dimensions beyond, namely the celestial spheres (heaven) and the chthonic or subterranean ones (underworld). In the shamanic traditions of central Siberia and Mongolia, the shaman climbs the World Tree in a state of trance (the tree is usually a birch, because *Taxus* cannot survive the long continental winters in Asia) to access the spirit world, to which there are many layers and regions. Ancient texts from India, Persia and Sumer also describe the World Tree as connecting all worlds and all life. Furthermore, the World Tree is the living, organic version of the cosmological 'world axis' or 'world pillar', which represents the centre of space and simultaneously the centre of time. The centre of space, or Earth, is the crossroads where all paths to different dimensions meet; one does not need to go further – everything is 'here'. The centre of time is like the eye of a hurricane – it is stillness. Time revolves, but in the centre of movement is a gateway to eternity – all is 'now'. Throughout the world, and for millennia, people have created sanctuaries around venerated trees or sacred groves, aiming to give these concepts a physical expression. For example, the historic Buddha, the Indian prince Gautama Siddhartha, was able to chose such a tree sanctuary (a pipal tree, *Ficus religiosa*) to search for enlightenment some 2,600 years ago.[32]

The branch motif in Palaeolithic cave paintings at (*clockwise from top left*)
El Castillo, Puente Viesgo (Cantabria, Spain); Lascaux, Niaux and Marsoulas
(all France).

The Stone and Bronze Age origins of the World Tree can all be located within the geographical distribution of the yew. No other tree species is evergreen and also produces sweet liquid the colour of blood, has poisonous as well as healing properties, and defeats time with its extraordinary lifespan. Much in yew lore points to the World

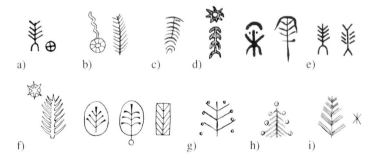

World Tree petroglyphs appear rather coniferous, even yew-like, during the late Stone Age and the Bronze Age. These examples are from a) Owens Valley; b) Blarisden, both USA; c) Slial na Calliaghe, Ireland; d) La Pileta, Le Zarzalon, Las Palomas, all Spain; e) Gezer, Israel; f) Susa, Persia (pre-Elamitic); g) Poland; h) Armenia; i) Dnjepr Valley, Russia.

Tree tradition, but anthropologists and historians of religion have not yet put two and two together. What are the reasons for the missing recognition of yew in this respect?

For one, yew worship and legends around the Mediterranean Sea had already begun to be marginalized during the Late Bronze and Iron Ages, reflecting the increasing domination of warrior and thunder-god cults, particularly in Greece and Rome. During the Middle Ages, most European yew stands disappeared, which put an end to local and regional yew traditions. For the last few centuries, the spiritual yew was simply *invisible* to the eyes of Christian European researchers: the 'tree of death' in British graveyards was not known to have links with any other religious tradition in the world. Classical written sources were already studded with dramatic mistranslations – for example, the Roman scholar Pliny (AD 23–79), not a botanist at all, took Theophrastus' entire passage on yew (Greek *mílos*), and assigned it to ash (Greek *melía*).[33] He also wrote that the Greeks called the monoecious holm oak *mílax* – which is another ancient Greek term for yew.[34] Ancient texts from Greece and the Near East often speak of 'cedar' when describing yew.[35] The sacred trees of the ancient Hebrews changed species during the various translations of the Old Testament into Latin, English and other languages, which had an indirect effect on obscuring yew even further.[36] Furthermore, old European texts talking about trees bearing 'apples' and 'acorns' were not recognized as descriptions of yew. Fortunately for us today, yew depictions in a sacred context go back to well before the age of writing; but most of the archaeological evidence has only been unearthed during the last few decades. There was also a morphological problem: with wild yews out of sight and the yew's branch layering in parks and churchyards usually neatly cut back, nobody could understand Classical references such as Ovid's when he describes the sacred grove of Ceres (the Roman Demeter) consisting of a huge tree that in itself was 'one grove' (*una nemus*), and from whose trunk blood streamed forth when it was hit with an axe in sacrilege.[37]

Coniferous twigs on a Babylonian pottery lid from Lagash, possibly from a vessel for offerings of incense or liquids.

There is one tradition, however, that has at all times connected yew and the World Tree: the Norse tradition regarding the Scandinavian World Tree named *Yggdrasil*. Alas, for the last few centuries, *Yggdrasil* has been interpreted as the 'world ash'. The reasons for this fundamental error in religious history are complex. Firstly,

there is the fact that all Nordic texts are written in the skaldic tradition. The skalds were the courtly poets of early medieval Scandinavia
and Iceland, and their craft extensively employed figurative language by means of metaphors and synonyms (*heiti*) and so-called
kennings. Kennings replace concrete, single-word nouns with abstract
phrases or compound words, all of which require deep background
knowledge of Nordic history and mythology. This was lacking in
British and German anthropologists of the eighteenth and nineteenth century, so the 'evergreen needle-ash' (*barraskr*) as a kenning
for the World Tree was taken literally as 'ash'. It hardly needs to be
pointed out that the broadleaved ash tree is neither evergreen nor
does it have needles.

The *vetgronstr vidr*, the 'wintergreenest' tree.

Additionally, the notion of a 'World Tree' conjures up expectations of a grand and stately tree shape. However, to the early anthropologists yew was known only as a low-growing, small tree never taller than 15 m (50 ft), often with twisted multiple trunks. The tall, monocormic, monumental yews such as those mentioned by Classical writers 2,000 years ago, and still existing in Turkey and the Caucasus, where they reach 20–40 m (65–131 ft) in height, had long disappeared from Europe.[38] The stately, majestic ash (*Fraxinus excelsior*) seemed a feasible choice.

There are two old Icelandic sources that call *Yggdrasil* plainly 'ash'. But do they really? The seer in the medieval text *Völuspa*, a principal source on Norse mythology, says: 'An *ask* I know there stands . . . showered with shining loam. From there come the dews that drop in the valleys' (stanza 19). The context here is obviously that of collecting a liquid, 'shining loam', and pouring it out again as dew in the valleys.[39] This is to say that the World Tree receives heavenly nourishment (ambrosia, nectar or honey mead in different traditions) and transmits it to the plants, animals and humans on Earth. In Icelandic, *ask/askr* can mean 'ash', but also denotes a traditional wooden soup bowl, sometimes with a lid and a handle.[40] Other Icelandic texts call the World Tree *vetgrønstr vidr*, 'wintergreenest tree', and *Laerad*, the 'glossy one'. These are all poetic descriptions that do not fit ash, because ash is not wintergreen and has no gloss. The above, however, exhausts the argument for the case of the ash as *Yggdrasil*.

The case for yew is stronger, particularly since the old documents have been revisited and retranslated since the 1990s. *Völuspa* (stanza 2) speaks of '*nío ívidiur, . . . miotvid mæran*', 'nine yew root giantesses, . . . under the ground' – giants, like the ancient Greek Titans, being archaic, later somewhat defamed, nature spirits, while *ívid* would normally be 'yew tree', but in the context of 'under the ground' becomes 'yew roots'. However, the key to understanding *Yggdrasil* is Heimdallr. By the Viking age, Heimdallr had developed into an anthropomorphic deity, a stout warrior guarding the rainbow bridge to the abode of the gods, but that image betrays Heimdall's ancient roots

– quite literally, because *heim* means 'world' and *dallr* is an old Icelandic word for 'tree'. Heimdallr is no anthropomorphic deity but the 'World Tree' itself. He guards no 'rainbow bridge' because as the world axis, he himself is the light-bridge to the divine world, brought forth by nine female yew root sisters. Another source confirms his origin: in *Heimdallargaldr*, 'Incantation of Heimdallr', he himself states that he is the son of nine mothers, all of whom are sisters. The poem *Hyndluliód* (stanza 35) describes him as 'one of the race of divine powers', born from nine *ívídia*.[41] Apart from this, one possible translation of *Yggdrasil* is 'yew column', analogous to *Ig-wano*, 'yew goddess',[42] and reminiscent of the Apulunas/Apollo columns mentioned

Laerad, the 'glossy one'.

The old Germanic
yew runes *eiwaz* and *yr*.

above. Furthermore, in another text,[43] *ívíðía*
is used as a metaphor for (a human lineage)
to bear numerous offspring – as prolific and
abundant as adventitious growth on yew (not
ash) roots. The composer of this Icelandic
saga draws directly on the mythology of his
people: *Voluspa* opens by addressing the audi-
ence as the 'hallowed seed, greater and hum-
bler, sons of Heimdallr'. In other words, all
humankind has descended from the World
Tree and its nine *ívíðía*.

It is no surprise, then, to find grave goods
made of yew in the *Yggdrasil* tradition, most
intriguingly the mysterious yew-wood buckets
found in countless Germanic graves in Den-
mark, Saxonia, Thuringia and Frankia, and also in a Merovingian
grave, two graves in Slovakia and two Anglo-Saxon graves in England.
They are receptacles for holding the heavenly dews that drop from
the World Tree.

At the heart of a national sanctuary at Uppsala, the old Swedish
capital, stood a huge evergreen tree, reported in the late eleventh
century and widely accepted today to have been a yew.[44] In the rune
alphabets, yew has two runes named after it, *eiwaz* and *yr*, which
symbolize transformation. Probably with the notion of the Norns
(the northern equivalent of the Greek Fates) sitting at the foot of the
World Tree casting the fates of humans every morning, yew sticks
were very popular for rune charms: a number of old runic talismans
have been found in the coastal regions of the North Sea, and they are
mostly made of yew wood. For example, a yew wand from AD *c.* 600
holds a spell to calm the storm and the waves of the sea, and the
inscription on a wand from the ninth century has been translated as
'Always carry this yew. It contains strength'.[45] Last but not least, the
rune *eiwahz* represents the yew tree and symbolizes death and rebirth,
while the ash tree has no rune ascribed to it.

The images of (three) wise old females (Norns, Fates) decreeing and prophesying beneath the sacred tree, and of the nine root mothers and mountain mothers (Muses) are striking parallels, bridging 2,000 miles and 3,000 years.

> *He who cannot be far-sighted,*
> *Nor three thousand years assay,*
> *Inexperienced stays benighted,*
> *Let him live from day to day.*
> JOHANN WOLFGANG VON GOETHE,
> *WEST-EASTERN DIVAN*

ten

Sacred Yew

ꕥ

Many sublime yews can be found at Buddhist temples and particularly at Shinto shrines in Japan. The Shinto faith acknowledges a superior or divine realm that nourishes and guides the visible world and human existence. Supernatural beings called *kami* act as guides or agents who oversee all aspects of nature and human life, and the *kami* reside in every living thing. In Shinto, all evergreen trees are considered sacred because they maintain their life during the winter and are therefore believed to partake in the divine realm in a special way. If, additionally, a tree is perceived to be the passage that a *kami* takes in coming down to Earth, it is designated as a *shinboku*, a sacred tree. To protect the tree, the place may be gently turned into a *jinja*, a 'shrine': a ceremonial *torii*, or sacred gateway, is set up in front of it and painted in the sacred colour, red. A special rope made of rice straw, a *nawa*, is tied around the tree, and *gohei*, paired strips of paper each torn in four places, are hung from the *nawa*.[1] The Hakusan Jinja yew tree, an example of such a tree, is about 13 m (43 ft) tall and has a girth of 6.1 m (20 ft). It was designated as a sacred tree in 1673 and has been protected ever since.

In Europe, too, yew had been a special tree since the dawn of civilization. When Christianity arrived it found a tree with deep links to the concepts of personal transformation, rebirth and immortality. Christianity adopted a part of this heritage, and simply replaced the concept of 'rebirth' with that of 'resurrection'.

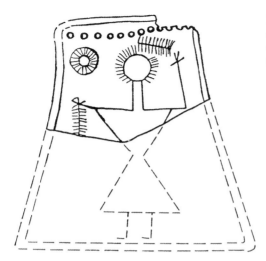

Female dancer with sacred branch. Pottery shard, Sardinia, late 5th millennium BC.

Some of the early monks in Ireland and Wales lived in ancient hollow yew trees, which served them as a home and shelter as well as an oratory – St Kevin, for example, is said to have lived in a hollow tree for seven years from about 510. As some hermitages eventually grew into flourishing churches or monasteries, they were named after the hospitable trees of their early history, such as Killure, Cell Iubhar, Cell-eo (all meaning 'church of the yew') and Killeochaille ('church of the yew wood'). Clonmacnoise had a huge yew tree, possibly planted by St Ciaran, which was struck by lightning in January 1149. St Columba (Columcille) is recorded as having preached under a large yew tree on the island of Bernera in the Hebrides. The Cistercian abbey of Iubhar Cinn Trágha, 'the yew tree at the head of the strand', modern Newry, Co. Down), was founded next to an old yew said to have been planted by St Patrick himself.[2] A group of Benedictine monks in Yorkshire founded Fountains Abbey in 1132, in a remote field overlooked by seven old yew trees. Until the first buildings were ready the monks took shelter, ate and prayed beneath these trees. In Ceridigion, Wales, the Cistercian colony at Ystrad Fflur (anglicized as Strata Florida) was originally home to a number of old yew trees – John Leland in the late 1530s mentions 'XXXIX great hue trees'.[3] Of these 39 trees, two still remain today. Like the Cistercians, the Knights Templar

Torii at Chuzenjii, Japan.

seem to have had a particular fondness for yew, and their paths cross in various places in Ireland (Iubhar Cinn Trágha), Scotland (Temple, Midlothian; Rosslyn) and France (La Couvertoirade). If there were no yews when they arrived at a place they planted some, as the Cistercians did at Waverley Abbey.

The tradition of planting yew trees in consecrated grounds has a spiritual as well as a practical meaning for Christianity. *Taxus baccata* is

Yew Shinto shrine at Hakusan Jinja, Japan.

one of the few native evergreens in the British Isles, and it comprises a well-rooted windbreak that protects a church building during winter storms. At the same time, its evergreen foliage is a comforting emblem of the continuity of life. In the absence of 'palm fronds', yew boughs and/or those of other evergreens constituted welcome decorations for church services – in fact, in some areas yew trees were still called 'palms' in the eighteenth and nineteenth centuries.[4]

Picturesque church entrance at Stow-on-the-Wold, Gloucestershire.

In the Middle Ages, many churchyards were not merely the locations for religious service, but also functioned as community centres, for the popular custom of mystery games or plays, which brought to life for the mostly illiterate audiences biblical stories re-enacted by the locals themselves. The main prop for the play about Adam and Eve was a 'paradise tree' – and in England the female yew was the first choice.[5] In Germany and Switzerland the cold continental winters inspired another tradition. For Christ's birth, people decorated a small yew as the paradise tree inside their homes – and hence the Christmas tree was born.

The great reverence for yew in medieval Wales can be glimpsed in the Laws of Hwel Da (tenth century), which set penalties for unauthorized felling or tree mutilation: 'A consecrated yew, its value is a

The statue of Adam and Eve was made in 1946 from a yew tree in St Paul's churchyard, Tiverton, and presented to the bishop of Bath and Wells in 1963.

pound . . . An oak, six score pence . . . A thorn-tree, sevenpence half-penny. Every tree after that, four pence.'[6] Back then, one pound was more than most people could ever earn in a lifetime. In Britain, many graveyards of Celtic or Saxon origin still have ancient yew trees, indicating that the transition to Christianity must have been comparatively smooth.

On the Continent the situation was different: the Frankish king Charlemagne, for example, utilized religious hegemony in his conquest of Saxonia. The Saxon tribes had an intertribal meeting place that served as a spiritual as well as a political centre: the Irminsul, a sacred tree or pillar representing the World Tree. The Saxon Wars began when Charlemagne invaded Saxon territory and destroyed the Irminsul in 772 or 773. The Saxons' resistance under their main leader, Widukind

The veteran yew at Waverley Abbey, Surrey, the first Cistercian House in England.

Fountains Abbey, drawing from Strutt's *Sylva Britannica* (1840).

('forest child'), lasted for more than 30 years, but eventually they surrendered to Charlemagne's relentless tactics (at one point he ordered the beheading of 4,500 Saxons for practising paganism after having been forcibly converted to Christianity). Hence the subsequent planting of yew trees in Saxonian (or Frankish) churchyards may not have been as abundant as in Saxon England.

Another reason why Britain has more churchyard yews than any other Christian country can probably be traced back to the Middle Ages, when rumours spread in Central Europe that yew preparations could be used for home abortions (many women actually died due to their improper use). If this should ever have moved churches to remove their yews we would not know, because no priest would have liked to commit to the annals the fact that such a thing as abortion happened in his community. In Britain, the folk medicine for this was juniper, and indeed the Scottish Church had junipers on many heaths cut down to prevent them from being used.

An old German proverb says 'Beneath yews no magic can persist',[7] which is why, in some areas, *Taxus* was quite popular for churchyard

Charlemagne's
destruction of the
Saxon World Pillar,
illustration from 1882.

hedges, to keep out ghosts. Another development took place in southern Europe, mainly France, when the pre-Christian places of worship of 'yew-goddesses' like Aphrodite or Artemis were converted to serve the Virgin Mary. Later, during the twelfth and thirteenth centuries, when the veneration of the Virgin Mary and female saints increased significantly,[8] Mary also became the patroness of the Cistercian Order and the Knights Templar. In another strand of development, the underworld aspects of female divinity, like black Kybele, or Aphrodite *Melaenis* (the 'black one'), also found a way of integration into Christianity, and brought forth a phenomenon that has puzzled Christian researchers ever since: the worship of the Black Madonna.[9] Le Puy en Velay (Haute-Loire) in France has been an important religious site for millennia. A Romanesque cathedral for the Black Virgin has replaced a church that was originally built *around* a prehistoric dolmen. The site was once dedicated to the Celtic goddess Ana, who locally was called *día Ana*, 'goddess Ana' or Romanized, Diana. Today

Traditional Madonna shrine inside the ancient yew at La Haye-de-Routot, Eure department, France. Girth 10.39 m (in 2000).

the hill of volcanic rock is also crowned by the colossal statue of Notre-Dame de France.

The only old yew woodland to have survived the Middle Ages in France is at Ste Baume in Provence. The age of the oldest yews there

LA-HAYE-DE-ROUTOT (Eure). - L'If Ste-Anne

Old postcards reveal no significant changes in the tree during the entire
20th century.

has been estimated at 800 years. It is a mixed yew-beech forest of
341 acres (138 ha) on the slopes beneath the limestone precipice
containing the sacred cave of Mary Magdalene. Goddess worship at
Ste Baume is considered to go back to the Neolithic period. When

Mary Magdalene's ascension above the yew wood at Ste Baume, Provence, France
(post-medieval drawing).

Phocaean Greeks founded the nearby city of Massilia (modern Marseille)
in about 600 BC, they dedicated Ste Baume to the goddess Artemis.[10]

In Asia, the goddess of mercy is Kuan Yin, 'She who hears the cries
of the world'. Before the Communist revolution, the old name for yew
in the mountainous areas of southwestern China was *Kuan Yin sha*,

'the conifer of the goddess of mercy'. Devotion to Kuan Yin – mostly without yew associations – spread eastwards across China, and is also very popular in Hong Kong, Taiwan and Korea today. In Japan, however, where she is known as Kannon, and can be found in Buddhist, Taoist and Shinto sacred sites (and homes) alike, the old yew link re-emerged: in Hida her statues are carved from *ichii*, the wood of yew.[11]

eleven

Threatened Yew

❧

Historically, the human impact on landscape and vegetation began to leave its marks in the fifth millennium BC, but the first large-scale deforestation occurred in Central Europe during the 600 years beginning *c.* 1150 BC. Due to human population pressure, agriculture and pasture, old-growth forests disappeared, and most yew populations were entirely destroyed by the trade in longbows. In North America, less than 5 per cent of the old-growth forests is left, with most of it having been destroyed as recently as the twentieth century. In Indonesia and other parts of Asia, large-scale deforestation only began some four decades ago. Whenever clear-felling is carried out within the geographical distribution area of *Taxus*, its scattered stands in the forest disappear – silently. There are no reports, inventories or statistics.

In the early 1960s, however, a worldwide hunt for yew trees began. After half a millennium of silence, *Taxus* bounced back into the political arena when a tumour-active compound was found in the bark of the Pacific yew in the northwestern United States in 1964, and identified and named in September 1966. In need of yew bark for chemical and later clinical trials, the NCI (National Cancer Institute) began to cooperate with the US Forest Service. At first, supply was not a problem because the timber industry in the Pacific West of North America was constantly clear-felling old-growth forests of conifers such as Douglas fir, Sitka spruce and Western cedar, trees of enormous commercial value. The smaller trees and

Veteran yew at
Kingley Vale, Sussex.

shrubs of the understorey had no value, and after the clear-cut they
were burned in so-called slash-piles. In the 1960s, yew was nothing
but an unvalued and unwanted 'trash tree', and even trunks more
than 500 years old could be found on the slash-piles.[1] The NCI's
yew scouts simply had to synchronize with the felling activities and
go into the forests to bark-strip the yew trees. However, as chemical
trials and animal testing continued promisingly, the NCI needed ever-
increasing amounts of bark. Because 12 kg (26 lb) of dried bark produces only 0.5 g of pure paclitaxel (0.004 per cent of weight),[2] tens
of thousands of trees needed to be bark-stripped. During the following three decades demand for bark continued to rise exponentially:
106 kg (234 lb) of yew material in April 1966; about 1,350 kg (2,976
lb) of dried bark in spring 1967; 39,000 kg (85,980 lb) in 1990;

725,000 kg (1,598,350 lb) in 1991, and the same amount again in 1992,[3] the year when paclitaxel finally achieved official approval as a marketable drug for human cancer chemotherapy in the USA. With the prospect of selling the drug to millions of cancer patients, the demand was to stay at this astronomical level – and increase even more. Where should all the yew material come from? A national conflict was dawning.

In the 1980s conservation of the last remaining areas of old-growth Pacific rainforest, of which yew is an integral part, became a key issue for the environmental movement in the USA. The Franklin Report,[4] commissioned by the Forest Service and published in 1981, contributed to the rising awareness of complex ecosystems and specialized habitats. It was the first in-depth study of old-growth forests in America, and in resisting a simple definition but instead taking an ecosystem approach and describing the forest in its entirety ('An old-growth forest is much more than simply a collection of large trees'), the report laid the foundations for what became 'New Forestry': the approach to managing younger forests by recreating certain old-growth characteristics. However, the concept was just a new idea, while the reality out there looked as old-fashioned as ever: clear-felling without any thoughts about ecosystems, endangered species or sustainability. The awakening ecological movement campaigned for the Pacific virgin forests, and the Pacific yew and the endemic spotted owl became iconic symbols. The conflict was hyped up by some media as a battle 'between saving the environment and saving lives',[5] thus creating a rift between the ecological movement and public opinion, a black-and-white drama that made headlines and promised to sell papers for some time to come. The ecological movement responded by stating that it did not put trees before human lives, but that by completely destroying the forests there would soon be no more yews left to obtain medicine from anyway.

Historically, there is a parallel here. Following events in Germany and England a century before, this was the third time that the yew tree was present in the birth processes of nature conservation. In

1911, the English botanist Sir Arthur George Tansley (1871–1955) and his German colleague Professor Drude had met at the impressive ancient yew grove at Kingley Vale in Sussex. The realization that there was a lack of conservation for these trees had been one of the precursors that had led Sir Arthur to found the British Ecological Society. In the 1880s, the botanist Hugo Conwentz (1855–1922) had become concerned about the yew populations of western Prussia (modern Poland) and subsequently was the first to campaign for areas of nature conservation in continental Europe.[6]

In the United States, the public controversy about the old-growth forests, the yew and paclitaxel grew through the 1980s, and so did the pressure on the NCI and the Forest Service. One ray of hope occurred in 1988, when the French chemist Pierre Potier co-published the first method to semi-synthesize an almost-identical tumour-active compound, docetaxel, from yew *foliage*. American chemists immediately set to work to create a similar solution and were successful in the space of a few years. This semi-synthesis from leaves promised a sustainable form of supply because the trees do not necessarily have to be killed for it. Pierre Potier (1934–2006) had set the wheels in motion that would save thousands of trees and even more human lives.

Development of paclitaxel semi-synthesis was, however, still under way when paclitaxel harvested from the bark received its official approval in 1992. Leading up to that date, the NCI passed the patent for the compound to a private company. Together with the formula for paclitaxel, the pharma giant Bristol-Myers Squibb received the exclusive rights to harvest the bark of endangered yew trees on United States territory. The US government was criticized for giving away the results of three decades of (expensive) research as soon as profits could begin to repay the investment of public funding. The public had paid for the development – with taxes and with the loss of trees – and a private company would now make the profits. So it did: only six years later, the company's product, Taxol®, had become the bestselling anti-cancer drug ever, with world sales of

Himalayan yew in
Northern India, 1989.

$1.2 billion. In 2003, the annual turnover in the USA alone had grown
to $3 billion.[7]

The early taxane industry also inherited two 'problems': increasing ecological criticism inside the USA, and the fact that Pacific yew
populations were becoming scarcer anyway. The beginning of the
technological shift from bark to leaf extraction did not solve the
second problem. Hence, while everyone looked at the trees in America,
the harvesting of wild trees was simply shifted to Asia, primarily India
and China. Since 1992, enormous amounts of yew biomass have been
exported from the countries bordering the Himalayas for various
Western pharmaceutical companies. During the 1990s, semi-synthesis
from the leaves was still more expensive than extraction from the bark,
so these Asian trees were not sustainably harvested for their foliage,
but were felled and stripped of everything as if there was no tomorrow.

Within a few years, 90 per cent of Himalayan yews had disappeared. What saved the Asian yews from total extinction, albeit almost too late, was the fact that the Convention for International Trade in Endangered Species (CITES) included the Himalayan yew in its list of endangered species in 1999. As international trade was the main cause of its disappearance, the CITES used its power to curb the trade and hence the over-exploitation. However, illegal logging still goes on in many countries. Various conservation organizations – among them the World Wide Fund for Nature (WWF), the International Union for the Conservation of Nature (IUCN) and the Species Survival Commission – presently consider Himalayan yew as one of the ten most threatened species.[8]

The vast scale of the destruction of yew populations in America and Asia for the needs of the pharmaceutical industry can only be compared with the ecological results of the European 'longbow mania'. The only difference is that what took four centuries in medieval Europe took only twenty years in America and Asia.

The way forward seemed to be plantations of yew trees on an industrial scale. Indeed, the first research programmes into yew plantations were launched in 1987, and in 1996, *Taxus* plantations in Oregon and Washington State were estimated to contain 20–25 million plants. Additional American plantations are located in Taiwan and the Philippines. Other countries, for example Korea, have begun national yew pharmaceutics industries. China has, of course, initiated plantations on a scale that dwarfs everything else. It has been estimated that by 2010 global plantations reached 100 million young yew trees.[9] Unfortunately, a new problem dawns on the horizon. For these plantations, multitudes of single plants have been propagated from a comparatively small number of seedlings, via cuttings from parent plants. This effectively makes them clones, albeit they are not genetically engineered as such. In a few years, millions of plantation clones will reach sexual maturity, and the trees with male flowers will produce pollen that is bound to interfere with the natural regeneration of the small numbers of remaining native yew trees in

Asia, further jeopardizing the genetic diversity of the various Asian subspecies of yew.

A quite different approach has been adopted in Canada. Here, a pilot project of the Ministry of Natural Resources in Quebec favours harvesting methods of sustainable amounts of yew foliage (cropping the top eight inches of branches every three years) in natural mixed forests.[10] The challenge, of course, is that such a gentle approach needs to be competitive. As Emmanuelle Neyroumande from the WWF's Paris office puts it:

> the same molecule will cost a lot less if it is produced in conditions that aren't so heavily controlled, such as in Asia, in Afghanistan, Pakistan, Vietnam or elsewhere, compared to a molecule that has been manufactured in a very regulated way in Canada or North America . . . It's obvious that all the efforts to really try and integrate ecology, using the leaves, renewability, plantations etc., are at a disadvantage economy-wise compared to a sort of unfair competition.[11]

A project at Fredericton University, New Brunswick, Canada, responded to this situation by aiming to 'optimize' the plant to make it grow faster and with higher taxane yield. Once found, the 'elite yew' is planned to be cloned as GMOs (genetically modified organisms).[12]

The yew has become a strategic natural resource, subjected to the extreme tensions of a deregulated world market.[13] Most of the old-growth forests in Asia, America and Europe have disappeared. This makes the last old yew forests in Turkey and the Caucasus, as well as the scattered ancient yews of Britain, a world heritage that is all the more precious because it has become so rare. So what is the current situation? What is left and how is it protected?

The IUCN Red List of Threatened Species lists yew as Least Concern (LC) because there are enough yew trees in the world. However, due

Large-scale yew plantation, Chinese advertising leaflet.

to general deforestation worldwide, and to the hunt for taxanes in particular, the status of yew varies from vulnerable to endangered in many regions of the world. In some regions of its original distribution, *Taxus* is critically endangered or already extinct.

In North America, millions of Pacific yews were felled for the taxanes in their bark during the 1980s and '90s. A large proportion of really old yews on federal lands was harvested, too, but a fair number remains in protected areas and relatively inaccessible locations far from roads. Since taxanes are now being produced more economically by growing yews in nurseries, the wild trees are at last being left alone. In the USA the species is not threatened because of abundant regeneration, and now federal lands have a mandate to encourage species diversity in regenerated stands of harvested trees. There is no special protection status for yews on federal lands. Although the total number of yews remains large, 85 to 90 per cent of these have stems no larger than 10 cm (4 in) in diameter. Many are just shrubs and not trees. The *Taxus* populations after the paclitaxel disaster are incredibly young.

In 1991 it was estimated that yew in Idaho, Montana, Washington, Oregon and California was present on between 3.2 and 3.7 million acres, according to the Forest Service and the Bureau of Land Management. The Fish and Wildlife Service, however, estimated that yew was present on no more than 1.2 million acres, explaining the discrepancy with the fact that the Forest Service had also considered areas that had already been cut, that is, secondary and tertiary growth forests. *Taxus* is, however, a distinct species of old-growth forests, and its numbers decline with their disappearance. The Fish and Wildlife Service argued that many yews had not even reached sexual maturity and hence could not contribute to the perpetuation of the species, and never will if they are repeatedly cut down (in general clear-fellings every 50 to 70 years) before they reach maturity.[14] If American parents want to show their children an ancient yew, they have three choices: search in the remote locations of the Pacific Northwest; visit a British churchyard yew; or wait at least 500 years until woodland populations in nature reserves have matured.

Regarding Asia, the Convention for International Trade in Endangered Species (CITES) finally included the Himalayan yew in its list in 1999 – after India had just lost 90 per cent of its yew trees to the international pharmaceutical demand in only seven years. Since then, exporting Himalayan yew has been forbidden, but in spite of this illegal trade still continues. Various conservation organizations – among them the WWF, IUCN and Species Survival Commission – presently consider yew in the Himalayas as one of the ten most threatened species.[15] This tree is also on the national list of endangered species in China and Vietnam; it reached a critical low point in Tibet in 1999 (WCMC).[16]

No data regarding Japanese forestry are available to the author, but the old and ancient yews in Shinto shrines enjoy strong protection. Furthermore, the priests can apply for an additional national protection – which is usually a smooth act because many administrators in government are also followers of Shinto. The sacred Kunimi yew, for example, 19 m (62 ft) tall, with a girth of about 7 m (23 ft), and estimated to be between 700 (Environmental Agency data) and 1,000 (other sources) years old, became a Natural Monument on 1 November 1967. The advantage of the Japanese scenario is that in Shinto, the trees themselves are *shinboku*, 'sacred', while in Christian

礼门红豆杉

2009
[农历己丑年]
HAPPY NEW YEAR

周宁县礼门乡旅游资源十富，风生态资源完好，被专家学者誉为"闽东的西双版纳"。境内大碑村现存五株千年红豆杉，其中最大树龄已达壹千五百余年，堪称"中华红豆杉王"。除此以外，尚有后垄村百余株野生红豆杉群，亦为自然之罕见奇观。

中共周宁县礼门乡委员会
周宁县礼门乡人民政府

09-350902-13-0534-000 宁德市邮政函件局发布

Such old yews are now very rare in the Republic: New Year's card from China.

The Kunimi yew, Nagano, Japan.

churchyards in Britain, the trees just happen to stand on 'consecrated ground', a situation that, when in doubt, favours the building or anything else but the tree.

In continental Europe, yew is generally protected. Additionally, it is on the national Red List in Germany and Austria. Similarly, yew is considered to be an endangered species in Spain, and no parts can be removed from the tree.

In Italy, too, it is completely forbidden to cut *Taxus baccata* anywhere on the Italian peninsula, including the islands, since the species is considered rare and endangered. (The only exceptions are the mixed stands in the Alps, where there is no restriction to the silvicultural management of the yew, and the species is also more abundant.) Furthermore, many yew stands (mixed beech-yew-woods) on peninsular Italy are protected as Sites of Community Importance

(SCI), Regional Parks or Regional Reserves (for example Monti Simbruini Regional Park and Natural Regional Reserve of Monte Genzana Alto Gizio). In Italy, a Natural Reserve/Park is an area where special ecosystems for biodiversity conservation are found; here, forest management is generally allowed. The level of protection of Regional Reserves/Parks is in agreement with the European Habitat Directive 92/43/CE. The ancient yew population in Foresta Umbra is protected as an SCI (Foresta Umbra) and as a National Park (Parco Nazionale del Gargano).[17]

In Spain, yew woods and their associated ecosystems are protected as Priority Habitats 9580 UE; additionally, several forests are in National Parks and/or Reserve Areas. The ancient and veteran churchyard yews in northern Spain are catalogued and are just receiving a special management plan. In the rest of Spain, special solitary yews outside churchyards are also catalogued for longevity or uniqueness, or as 'monument' yews.[18]

The oldest yew forest in Germany, Paterzell, has been protected as a 'national natural monument' since 1913, and is now protected by the Federal Nature Conservation Act. Other yew woods in Germany

Signpost at the sacred Kunimi yew, a Natural Monument since 1967.

Natural Monument metal plaque on an old yew trunk in Bavaria.

have national protection, and some of them are located in Flora-Fauna-Habitats under European guidelines (Natura 2000). Additionally, solitary veteran yews often bear a small metal plaque with the words 'Natural Monument' or 'National Monument'.[19]

In Slovenia, yew became a protected species in 1976. Forest reserves (virgin forests) and national parks protect woodlands, and conservation of forest genetic resources has long been an integral part of sustainable forest management based on the Forest Act of 1993.[20]

In Albania, over 892,050 acres (361,000 ha) of forest, including mixed yew woods, are classified as Protected Areas, classified according to the IUCN criteria. That represents 12½ per cent of the country's total surface.[21]

In Iran, the yew woods (32 acres/13 ha with up to 32 per cent yew) in the vast Hycernian Forest by the Caspian Sea in the north of the country are now protected as nature reserves. Yew is also in the Red Data Book of Iran.[22]

The largest and most important populations of old and ancient yews are in the stewardship of four countries: Turkey, Russia, Georgia (Caucasus) and Great Britain.

In Turkey, hundreds of ancient yews (no inventory has yet been made) are located in the temperate forests along the southern Black Sea coast. The prevailing religion (Islam), the forestry commission and the legal executive are aware of their cherished heritage. The forest is protected by the National Park status of the area (494 acres/200 ha) and the local forest authority is working to improve the protection status to an internationally acknowledged Biosphere Reserve according to the guidelines of the IUCN.[23]

The Caucasus Mountains host 130 yew stands, according to Russian data. Only three are located in Georgia, because – although *Taxus* had been fully protected since the decree of the Christian Queen Tamara in the twelfth century – the country lost almost all its yews in the nineteenth century. The ancient yew forest in the remote Bazara Gorge was discovered during a forest inventory in 1923/4, and designated as a Protected Forest by the Soviet government as early as April 1928. With some interruptions the area has been protected since that time. Today, the Strict Nature Reserve level (IUCN Protected Area Management Category 1) applies to 7,492 acres (3,032 ha), including 586 acres (237 ha) of yew forest; 210,000 yews are under 200 years old and 13,000 over 200 years, and there are clusters of

Monumental yew 'The Patriarch' at the Bazara Reserve, Georgia.

old trees with an estimated average age of 800 years. The oldest tree, 'the patriarch', commonly referred to as 2,000 years old, was verified in 2010 to be about 1,530 years old. Adjoining Bazara to the west is the Ilto Managed Reserve, founded in April 2003, and complying with IUCN Category IV. It is bigger than the Bazara Reserve but has fewer yews. The Ilto Reserve was founded exclusively to protect the yew trees, which have been on the Red List in Georgia since 1982, and the species is classified by the IUCN as 'Vulnerable' in Georgia. Nevertheless, a licence was given in 2001 to a Georgian-American company, Natex Gorgia, to collect yew foliage for paclitaxel production from the forests bordering the Ilto Reserve. The company broke many conditions of the contract (for example, only 30-cm-long twigs were allowed to be cut, but instead whole trees were felled, including some old trees inside the reserve), and in three years exported 420 tons of yew foliage from the area, although the true dark-figure amount is not known. This situation was brought to a stop by the persistent campaigning of an environmental group, the Nature Friends of Georgia. The third Georgian yew population is also a protected reserve, Kidrischi in Acharia province. Since early 2011, the Georgian Ministry of the Environment has a specialist group preparing an application for World Heritage status for the Bazara Reserve with UNESCO.[24]

The situation of the Russian yew populations cannot presently be assessed. In far eastern Siberia, the emphasis is on clear-felling and exporting timber, hence no figures are published. In the Caucasus, all yew stands had been organized well and responsibly by the Forest Department of the University of Sochi, but since about 2005 access to the mountain reserves has been impossible due to the persistent conflict with Chechnya. Armed gangs and guerillas are living in the wooded mountains, and Chechnya has become one of the world's most densely land-mined regions. The yew reserves are encompassed by prohibited military areas.[25]

In the United Kingdom, 1,280 veteran and ancient yews are currently on the AYG database, the vast majority of them in churchyards (72 per cent). There is no comprehensive national legal protection at all, only erratic fragmented cover. Very few single yew trees are protected by a TPO (Tree Preservation Order) or because

Yew stump at Goetre, Monmouthshire, felled in 1973, girth 6.87 m.

Yew seedling.

they are located in a designated conservation area. Since 2013, some of the sacred yew trees of Britain have been represented on the worldwide database of sacred natural sites (www.mappingthesacred.org), a project of the Open University and the University of Oxford. The Church of England, however, is slow to recognize its botanical heritage – it is still possible for an ancient churchyard yew to be felled, even when that tree is thought to be safeguarded by the churchyard's Conservation Area status.

With only 9 per cent forest cover (for comparison: Germany 32 per cent, Slovenia 60 per cent), England is one of the most deforested countries in the world (Wales and Scotland have a few per cent more).[26] Nothing is left of the ancient virgin beech-yew-woods and oak-yew-woods that once covered most of the land. In an abstract way, the remaining true ancient 'forest' of Britain – *representing about 80 per cent of the oldest trees in all of Western Europe* – could be seen in the above-mentioned 1,280 yew trees scattered in 590 churchyards and some 280 wilderness locations, parks and gardens.

With the vast majority of yew populations in North America, Asia and Europe now gone, Britain has become a Noah's Ark for the gene pools of ancient yew trees. Despite this, the UK Forestry Commission shows no intentions to replant yew trees on any scale, and the Church of England does not seem to engage with ecological concerns about God's creation. Still we continue to lose irreplaceable trees of unknown great age – trees that hold unfathomable scientific (genetic) importance and perhaps the future cure for other diseases; trees that continue to make a unique contribution to the cultural and spiritual wealth of a country.

> *Don't you know that the forests are the life of a country?*
> ANCIENT BABYLONIAN INSCRIPTION[27]

Timeline

200 million years ago	*Palaeotaxus rediviva*, the predecessor of the genus *Taxus*, is distributed widely across the global landmass that has not yet separated into continents
140 million years ago	*Marskea jurassica* (formerly *Taxus jurassica*) contains most of the characteristics of the modern species
15 million years ago	The oldest record so far of the modern species *Taxus baccata*
400,000–367,000 years ago	The greatest yew density in natural history appears in the warm, oceanic climate of the Hoxnian interglacial
300,000–200,000 years ago	Neanderthals manufacture the oldest yew artefact we know today: a hunting spear found at Clacton-on-Sea in Essex
45,000 years ago	First possible encounter of *Homo sapiens* and *Taxus baccata*, in Asia Minor
17,500 years ago	Oldest known depiction of yew branch in the cave paintings of Lascaux, France
7,800–7,200 years ago	After the Ice Age, *Taxus* reappears north of the Alps, in Central Europe (Germany)
5000 BC	*Taxus* reappears in postglacial Britain
c. 3300 BC	Yew longbow of the 'Ice Man' from the Tyrolean Alps
c. 1750 BC	Yew as a sacred tree praised in Hittite cuneiform tablets from Anatolia (Turkey)

c. 600 BC	Greek settlers in southern France found Marseille and dedicate the ancient yew wood of Ste Baume to Artemis
c. 300 BC	Theophrastus reports the main sanctuary of Artemis in Greece as being located in a yew grove
1st–3rd centuries AD	Scandinavian bow makers develop the yew composite bow, the forerunner of the medieval 'great war bow'
6th century	St Columba (Columcille) preaches under a large yew tree on the island of Bernera in the Hebrides, Scotland
772–3	Charlemagne's invasion of Saxonia and destruction of the Irminsul ends the history of the sacred yew among continental Saxons
c. 1200	Queen Tamara of Iberia (modern Georgia) decrees the yews in her country protected from commercial interests
1274–1307	During his reign, Edward I gradually incorporates yew longbowmen into the English army
15th and 16th centuries	European yew longbow stave exports to England at their heights
1589	End of the yew stave trade; no yew tree of size left in the Alps
26 October 1595	Queen Elizabeth I has to replace the longbows of the army with shotguns due to shortage of yew wood
December 1798	First description of a Christmas tree, a yew in Germany, by the English poet Samuel Taylor Coleridge
1906	Hugo Conwentz in Germany establishes the first nature conservation area in the world, to protect unique yew forests in Poland
May 1964	In the United States, a compound with anti-tumour properties is discovered in the bark of yew trees; at first hundreds, later millions of yews are destroyed for their bark

1988	The French chemist Pierre Potier co-publishes the first method to semi-synthesize a tumour-active compound, docetaxel
1992	First official approval of marketable drug for human cancer chemotherapy in the USA; UK follows in 2004/05
1992–1999	Due to the pharmaceutical rush for raw yew materials, India loses 90 per cent of its *Taxus* population; yew becomes endangered in many Asian countries
1998–1999	In Britain, the Yews for the Millennium campaign offers yew cuttings from ancient churchyard yews to church parishes, and later also to schools and public bodies
2003	Taxol® sales still going strong, reaching $3 billion in the U.S. alone
2005	Ancient Yew Group (AYG) founded in Britain to raise awareness of ancient yews

References

Introduction

1 C. Leuthold, 'Die Pflanzensoziologische und Ökologische Stellung der Eibe (*Taxus baccata* L.), in der Schweiz: Ein Beitrag zur Wesenscharakterisierung des "Ur-Baumes" Europas', *Der Eibenfreund*, 4 (Markgroeningen, 1998), p. 364.

2 Harold Saxton Burr at Yale, see Fred Hageneder, *Yew: A History* (Stroud, 2007), p. 32.

3 Rajda's full study is documented in Hageneder, *Yew*, chap. 17, for which it was commissioned.

4 Leuthold, 'Die Pflanzensoziologische und Ökologische Stellung der Eibe, pp. 349–71.

5 Thomas Scheeder, *Die Eibe* (Taxus baccata *L.): Hoffnung Für ein Fast Verschwundenes Waldvolk* (Eching, 1994), p. 50.

1 Early Yew

1 A. Brande, 'Die Eibe in Berlin Einst und Jetzt', *Der Eibenfreund*, 8 (Markgroeningen, 2001), pp. 24–43, 24.

2 Louis Emberger, *Les Plantes Fossiles* (Paris, 1968), p. 583.

3 Fred Hageneder, *Yew: A History* (Stroud, 2007), p. 14.

4 P. A. Thomas and A. Polwart, 'Biological Flora of the British Isles. *Taxus baccata* L.', *Journal of Ecology*, 91 (2003), p. 513.

5 Brande, 'Die Eibe in Berlin Einst und Jetzt', pp. 24–43, 25.

6 A. Brande, 'Postglaziale *Taxus*-Nachweise und Waldtypen in den Nördlichen Kalkalpen (Niederösterreich)', *Der Eibenfreund*, 10 (Markgroeningen, 2003), pp. 52–62, 58–9.

7 Brande, 'Die Eibe in Berlin Einst und Jetzt', pp. 24–43, 26.

8 Thomas, 'Biological Flora of the British Isles', p. 514.

9 Fred Hageneder, *The Spirit of Trees: Science, Synthesis and Inspiration* (Edinburgh and New York, 2000), p. 57.

2 Botanical Yew

1 Ulrich Pietzarka, 'Zur Ökologischen Strategie der Eibe (*Taxus baccata* L.): Wachstums- und Verjüngungsdynamik', doctorate (Dresden, 2005), 3.2.2.

2 Fred Hageneder, *Yew: A History* (Stroud, 2007), p. 19, table 3.

3 Ibid., p. 21, table 5.

4 A. Pisek et al., 'Kardinale Temperaturbereiche der Photosynthese und Grenztemperaturen des Lebens der Blätter Verschiedener Spermatophyten. 1. Temperaturminimum der Nettoassimilation, Gefrier- und Frostschadensbereiche der Blätter', *Flora*, 157 (1967), pp. 239–64.

5 Ibid.

6 R. K. Szaniawski, 'An Outline of Yew Physiology', in S. Bartkowiak et al., *The Yew*: Taxus baccata L. (Warsaw, 1978), p. 61.

7 A. Dumitru, 'Die Eibe (*Taxus baccata* L.): Eine Botanisch-ökologische Sowie Medizinische und Kulturhistorische Betrachtung', diploma in Forest Science (Munich, 1992), p. 74.

8 L. Núñez-Regueira et al., 'Calorific Values and Flammability of Forest Species in Galicia. Continental High Mountainous and Humid Atlantic Zones', *Bioresource Technology*, 61 (1997), pp. 111–19.

9 A. T. Groves and O. Rackham, *The Nature of Mediterranean Europe: An Ecological History* (New Haven, CT, and London, 2001), pp. 218, 236.

10 W. N. Stewart, *Palaeobotany and the Evolution of Plants* (Cambridge, 1983).

11 Hageneder, *Yew*, p. 12, referring to the *Strasburger Lehrbuch der Botanik,* 35th edn (Heidelberg, 2002).

12 Ibid., p. 13.

13 Federico Vesella and Bartolomeo Schirone, 'Regeneration Processes and Sexual Behaviour of Yew Populations in Italy', *Der Eibenfreund*, 17 (Markgroeningen, 2011), pp. 69–84.

14 S. P. DiFazio, N. C. Vance and M. V. Wilson, 'Strobilus Production and Growth of Pacific Yew Under a Range of Overstorey Conditions in Western Oregon', *Canadian Journal of Forest Research*, 27 (1997), pp. 986–93; M. Hofmann, 'Das Naturwaldreservat Huckstein: Baumwachstum und Flora als Ausdruck Geomorphologischer Standortprägung', diploma (Göttingen, 1989); Thomas Scheeder, *Die Eibe (*Taxus baccata L.*): Hoffnung Für ein Fast Verschwundenes Waldvolk* (Eching, 1994); M. Worbes, M. Hofmann and A. Roloff, 'Wuchsdynamik der Baumschicht in Einem Seggen-Kalkbuchenwald in Nordwestdeutschland (Huckstein)', *Dendrochronologia*, 10 (1992), pp. 91–106; Pietzarka, 'Zur Okologischen Strategie der Eibe', 3.8.2, also 4.1.3.

15 See chap. 1, note 3.

16 Pietzarka, 'Zur ökologischen Strategie der Eibe', 4.1.10.

17 I. Löblein, *Einfluss von Innerstädtischen Bodenverhältnissen auf das Durchwurzelungsverhalten von Eiben*, Staatsexamen (Münster, 1995).

18 A. Hejnowicz, 'The Yew: Anatomy, Embryology and Karyology', in S. Bartkowiak et al., *The Yew*: Taxus baccata L. (Warsaw, 1978), pp. 43–4.

19 Dumitru, 'Die Eibe (*Taxus baccata* L.)', p. 62; M. Ballero et al., 'Analysis of Pharmaceutically Relevant Taxoids in Wild Yew Trees from Sardinia', *Fitoterapia*, 74 (2003), pp. 34–9.

20 P.J.A. Howard, D. M. Howard and L. E. Lowe, 'Effects of Tree Species and Soil Physico-chemical Conditions on the Nature of Soil Organic Matter', *Soil Biology and Biochemistry*, 30 (1998), pp. 285–97.

21 Hageneder, *Yew*, p. 35, diagram 1.

22 Szaniawski, 'An Outline of Yew Physiology', pp. 55–63.

23 Hageneder, *Yew*, p. 34.

24 O. A. Di Sapio, S. J. Gattuso and M. A. Gattuso, 'Morphoanatomical Characters of *Taxus baccata* Bark and Leaves', *Fitoterapia*, 68 (1997), pp. 252–60; D. Dempsey and I. Hook, 'Yew *(Taxus)* Species: Chemical and Morphological Variations', *Pharmaceutical Biology*, 38 (2000), pp. 274–80; P. A. Thomas and A. Polwart, 'Biological Flora of the British Isles. *Taxus baccata* L.', *Journal of Ecology*, 91 (2003); Scheeder, *Die Eibe* (Taxus baccata L.), p. 35; Pietzarka, 'Zur Okologischen Strategie der Eibe'.

25 Hejnowicz, 'The Yew: Anatomy, Embryology and Karyology', p. 41; Pietzarka, 'Zur ökologischen Strategie der Eibe', 4.1.9; Scheeder, *Die Eibe (Taxus baccata L*, p. 22.

26 Pietzarka, 'Zur ökologischen Strategie der Eibe', 3.2.2., 3.7.1.1., 3.7.2.

27 Ibid., 4.1.7., 3.8.1.4.

28 Ibid., 3.6.2.

29 Szaniawski, 'An Outline of Yew Physiology', pp. 55–63.

30 U. Leonhardt, M. Paul and H. Wolf, 'Eibenwald bei Schlottwitz', *Der Eibenfreund*, 5 (Markgroeningen, 1998), pp. 65–71. Compare Vesella, 'Regeneration Processes and Sexual Behaviour of Yew Populations in Italy', p. 80.

31 Thomas, 'Biological Flora of the British Isles', p. 503.

32 Norbert Frank, 'Eiben (*Taxus baccata* L.) im Bakony-Wald: Einst und Jetzt', *Der Eibenfreund*, 10 (Markgroeningen, 2003), pp. 20–25.

33 C. Cao, 'Untersuchungen zur Genetischen Variation und zum Genfluß bei der Eibe (*Taxus baccata* L.)', masters degree (Göttingen, 2002); A. Lewandowski et al., 'Genetic Structure of English Yew (*Taxus baccata* L.) in the Wierzchlas Reserve: Implications for Genetic Conservation', *Forest Ecology and Management*, 73 (1995), pp. 221–7; S. Thoma, 'Genetische Variation an Enzymgenloci in Reliktbeständen der Eibe (*Taxus baccata* L.)', diploma (Göttingen, 1992); S. Thoma, 'Genetische Unterschiede Zwischen Vier Reliktbeständen der Eibe (*T. b.* L.)', *Forst und Holz*, 50 (1995), pp. 19–24; S. Lange et al., 'Fremdpaarung im Wald: Das Liebesleben der Eibe', *Der Eibenfreund*, 9 (Markgroeningen, 2001), pp. 113–16; Pietzarka, 'Zur Okologischen Strategie der Eibe', 4.1.2.

34 Vesella, 'Regeneration Processes and Sexual Behaviour of Yew Populations in Italy', pp. 69–84. Also personal communication with Prof. Schirone.

35 O. Kirchner et al., *Lebensgeschichte der Blütenpflanzen Mitteleuropas*, vol. 1 (Stuttgart, 1908), pp. 60–78; Hubert Rössner, 'Paterzeller Eibenwald:

Erinnerungen, Beobachtungen, Vermutungen', in M. Kölbel and O. Schmidt, eds, 'Beiträge zur Eibe', *Berichte aus der Bayrischen Landesanstalt für Wald und Forstwirtschaft*, 10 (1996), pp. 48–55.

36 Pietzarka, 'Zur Okologischen Strategie der Eibe', 4.1.5.

37 Thomas, 'Biological Flora of the British Isles', p. 503; Kirchner, *Lebensgeschichte der Blütenpflanzen Mitteleuropas*, pp. 60–78.

38 Pietzarka, 'Zur Okologischen Strategie der Eibe', 4.1.5.

39 Hejnowicz, 'The Yew: Anatomy, Embryology and Karyology', pp. 44–5; Hageneder, *Yew*, chap. 9.

40 B. Suszka, 'Generative and Vegetative Reproduction', in S. Bartkowiak et al., *The Yew: Taxus baccata L.* (Warsaw, 1978), pp. 87–102; C. M. Herrera, 'Vertebrate-dispersed Plants of the Iberian Peninsula: A Study of Fruit Characteristics', *Ecological Monographs*, 57 (1987), pp. 305–31.

41 Thomas, 'Biological Flora of the British Isles.', pp. 501–2.

42 R. Williamson, *The Great Yew Forest: The Natural History of Kingley Vale* (London, 1978), in P. A. Thomas, 'Biological Flora of the British Isles', *Journal of Ecology*, 91 (2003), p. 505.

43 United States Department of Agriculture, *Seeds of Woody Plants in the United States*, Agricultural Handbook 450 (Washington, DC, 1974); Suszka, 'Generative and Vegetative Reproduction', pp. 87–102.

44 Thomas, 'Biological Flora of the British Isles', p. 504.

45 Pietzarka, 'Zur Okologischen Strategie der Eibe', 3.1.1.2., 3.2.2., 3.4.2.

46 L. J. Kucera, 'Das Holz der Eibe', *Der Eibenfreund*, 4 (Markgroeningen, 1998), pp. 328–39, 330.

47 *Taxus* value from Thomas, 'Biological Flora of the British Isles', p. 500; other values from H. E. Desch, *Timber: Its Structure and Properties* (London, 1974).

48 A. Brande, 'Die Aeltesten Speere: Nicht aus Eibenholz', in *Der Eibenfreund*, 15 (Markgroeningen, 2009), pp. 205–6, 205.

49 Pietzarka, 'Zur Okologischen Strategie der Eibe', 3.8.2.

50 L. J. Kucera, 'Das Holz der Eibe', *Der Eibenfreund*, 4 (Markgroeningen, 1998), pp. 328–39, 332, table 1.

51 Personal communication with Dr U. Pietzarka, Saxonian State Arboretum, Tharandt, and site discussions with the German Yew Society, *Die Eibenfreunde*.

52 Thomas Scheeder, 'Zur Anthropogenen Nutzung der Eibe (*Taxus baccata* L.)', *Der Eibenfreund*, 7 (Markgroeningen, 2000), p. 68.

3 Social Yew

1 Ulrich Pietzarka, 'Zur Okologischen Strategie der Eibe (*Taxus baccata* L.): Wachstums- und Verjüngungsdynamik', doctorate (Dresden, 2005), 4.1., 4.2.

2 Ibid., 3.6.2.

3 Ibid., 4.2.1.

4 C. Leuthold, 'Die Okologische und Pflanzensoziologische Stellung der Eibe (*Taxus baccata*), in der Schweiz', *Veröffentlichungen des Geobotanischen Instituts der ETH*, 67 (Zurich, 1980), pp. 1–217.

5 P. A. Thomas and A. Polwart, 'Biological Flora of the British Isles. *Taxus baccata* L.', *Journal of Ecology*, 91 (2003), p. 492; A. Dumitru, 'Die Eibe (*Taxus baccata* L.): Eine Botanisch-ökologische Sowie Medizinische und Kulturhistorische Betrachtung', diploma in Forest Science (Munich, 1992), pp. 37–8.

6 Thomas, 'Biological Flora of the British Isles', p. 493.

7 Karlo Amirgulashvili, Iosebi (Soso) Turashvili and Tamar Nadiradze, 'Die Eibe (*Taxus baccata* L.) in Georgien, Insbesondere in der Bazara- und Ilto-Schlucht', *Der Eibenfreund*, 17 (Markgroeningen, 2011), pp. 137–46.

4 Ancient Yew

1 John White, *Estimating the Age of Large and Veteran Trees in Britain*, Information Note FCIN12 (Edinburgh, 1998), p. 2.

2 Doug Larson, 'Ancient Stunted Trees on Cliffs', *Nature*, 398 (1999).

3 Larson, personal correspondence with the author, August 2004.

4 Toby Hindson, 2003, *A Longitudinal Study of Monnington Walk* (unpub. MS).

5 Ulrich Pietzarka, 'Zur Okologischen Strategie der Eibe (*Taxus baccata* L.): Wachstums- und Verjüngungsdynamik', doctorate (Dresden, 2005), 4.1.3.

6 White, *Estimating the Age of Large and Veteran Trees in Britain*, p. 2.

7 At the Alan Mitchell Memorial Lecture 2000, see Fred Hageneder, *Yew: A History* (Stroud, 2007), chap. 19.

8 Interviewed by John Craven for a *Countryfile* programme on the BBC in 1991.

9 Zafer Kaya, 'Anit Agacin Hatira Defteri', *Kasnak Mesesi ve Türkiye Florasi Sempozyumu* (Istanbul, 1998); Fred Hageneder, 'Die Monumentaleiben der Türkei' [The Monumental Yews of Turkey], *Der Eibenfreund*, 13 (Markgroeningen, 2007), pp. 175–80.

10 Hageneder, *Yew*, p. 79.

11 Personal correspondence with the author, January 2004; quote from Mikhail Pridnya, '*Taxus baccata* in the Caucasus region', *Der Eibenfreund*, 9 (Markgroeningen, 2002), p. 152.

12 Dr A. K. Moir, interviewed by BBC1 North East and Cumbria in 'The Yew Detective (Featuring the Work of Paul Greenwood)', *Inside Out*, Series 6, Programme 2, 13 September 2004.

13 Hageneder, *Yew*, p. 79.

14 John Lowe, *The Yew-trees of Great Britain and Ireland* (London, 1897); R. Williamson, *The Great Yew Forest: The Natural History of Kingley Vale* (London, 1978).

15 Enzyme analysis performed by Dr M. Konnert at the Bavarian Bureau for Forestry, Teisendorf, Germany.

16 Pietzarka, 'Zur Okologischen Strategie der Eibe', 4.2.2.

17 Ibid., 4.1.11.

5 Hospitable Yew

1 P. A. Thomas and A. Polwart, 'Biological Flora of the British Isles. *Taxus baccata* L.', *Journal of Ecology*, 91 (2003), p. 508; R. G. Strouts and T. G. Winter, 'Diagnosis of Ill-health in Trees', *Research for Amenity Trees*, 2 (London, 1994).

2 Ibid.

3 A. Lewandowski et al., 'Genetic Structure of English yew (*Taxus baccata* L.) in the Wierzchlas Reserve: Implications for Genetic Conservation', *Forest Ecology and Management*, 73 (1995), pp. 221–7; J. Hassler, W. Schoch and R. Engesser, 'Auffällige Stammkrebse an Eiben (*Taxus baccata* L.) im Fürstenwald bei Chur (Graubünden, Schweiz)', *Schweizer Z. Forstwesen*, 155/9 (2004), pp. 400–403.

4 British Mycological Society Fungal Records Database (BMSFRD); in P. A. Thomas and A. Polwart, 'Biological Flora of the British Isles. *Taxus baccata* L.', *Journal of Ecology*, 91 (2003), p. 508.

5 B.W.L. de Vries and T. W. Kuyper, 'Holzbewohnende Pilze auf Eibe (*Taxus baccata*)', *Zeitschrift für Mykologie*, 56/1 (1990), pp. 87–94.

6 Ulrich Pietzarka, 'Zur Ökologischen Strategie der Eibe (*Taxus baccata* L.): Wachstums- und Verjüngungsdynamik', doctorate (Dresden, 2005), 3.4.2; R. W. Duncan, T. A. Bown, V. G. Marshall and A. K. Mitchell, 'Yew Big Bud Mite', *Forest Pest Leaflet*, 79 (Victoria, BC, 1997).

7 Margaret Redfern, 'The Life Cycle of the Yew Gall Midge, *Taxomyia taxi*', in Fred Hageneder, *Yew: A History* (Stroud, 2007), pp. 60–61.

8 Hageneder, *Yew*, p. 62; Thomas, 'Biological Flora of the British Isles', p. 508. See also Remi Coutin, 'Faune Entomologique de l'if, *Taxus baccata*', *Insectes*, 128/1 (2003), pp. 19–22. Rössner, personal communication.

9 Hageneder, *Yew*, chap. 14.

10 C. M. Smal and J. S. Fairley, 'The Fruits Available as Food to Small Rodents in Two Woodland Ecosystems', *Holarctic Ecology*, 3 (1980), pp. 10–18.

11 R. Williamson, *The Great Yew Forest: The Natural History of Kingley Vale* (London, 1978), p. 128.

12 Stanley Scher, 'Do Browsing Ungulates Diminish Avian Foraging? Studies of Woodpeckers in Forest Understorey Communities of Central Europe and Western North America Show Cause for Concern', *Der Eibenfreund*, 4 (Markgroeningen, 1998), pp. 411–19; Christian Wolf, 'Anmerkungen zu den Spechteinschlägen in der Eibe', *Der Eibenfreund*, 9 (Markgroeningen, 2002), pp. 169–74; Karl Huf, 'Specht hämmert im Kronthal Einzigartige Lochmuster in Eiben', *Der Eibenfreund*, 9 (Markgroeningen, 2002), pp. 174–5.

13 Wolf, 'Anmerkungen zu den Spechteinschlägen in der Eibe', p. 173.

14 R. M. Tittensor, 'Ecological History of Yew (*T. baccata* L.) in southern England', *Biological Conservation*, 17 (1980), pp. 243–65; C. M. Smal and J. S. Fairley, 'Food of Wood Mice and Bank Voles in Oak and Yew Woods in Killarney, Ireland', *Journal of Zoology*, 191 (1980), pp. 413–18.

15 P. E. Hulme, 'Natural Regeneration of Yew (*Taxus baccata* L.) Microsite, Seed or Herbivore Limitation', *Journal of Ecology*, 84 (1996), pp. 853–61; P. E. Hulme and T. Borelli, 'Variability in Post-dispersal Seed Predation in Deciduous Woodland: Relative Importance of Location, Seed Species, Burial and Density', *Plant Ecology*, 145 (1999), pp. 149–56; Hubert Rössner, 'Bemerkungen zur Diplomarbeit von Patrick Insinna (1999)', *Der Eibenfreund*, 8 (Markgroeningen, 2001), pp. 157–63.

16 S. Bartkowiak, (1978) 'Seed Dispersal by Birds', in S. Bartkowiak et al., *The Yew: Taxus baccata L.* (Warsaw, 1978), pp. 139–46.

17 Williamson, *The Great Yew Forest*, p. 83–4.

18 A. S. Watt, 'Yew Communities of the South Downs', *Journal of Ecology*, 14 (1926), pp. 282–316.

19 Tittensor, 'Ecological History of Yew', p. 260.

20 Thomas, 'Biological Flora of the British Isles'; Williamson, *The Great Yew Forest*; Jürg Hassler, 'Die Bedeutung der Tiere bei der Verbreitung der Eibensamen', *Der Eibenfreund*, 10 (Markgroeningen, 2003), pp. 118–20.

21 Hageneder, *Yew*, p. 53

22 Doug Larson et al., *The Urban Cliff Revolution: New Findings on the Origins and Evolution of Human Habitats* (Ontario, ON, 2004), p. 91.

23 A. Brande, 'Die Aeltesten Speere: Nicht aus Eibenholz', in *Der Eibenfreund*, 15 (Markgroeningen, 2009), pp. 205–6, quoting H. Godwin, *The History of the British Flora*, 2nd edn (Oxford, 1975), p. 116.

24 Brande, 'Die Aeltesten Speere', pp. 205–6; A. Brande, 'Die Eibe in Berlin Einst und Jetzt', *Der Eibenfreund*, 8 (Markgroeningen, 2001), pp. 24–43, 25.

6 Poisonous Yew

1 G. van Ingen, R. Visser, H. Peltenburg, A. M. van der Ark and M. Voortman, 'Sudden Unexpected Death Due to *Taxus* Poisoning: A Report of Five Cases, with Review of the Literature', *Forensic Science International*, 56 (1992), pp. 81–7.

2 R. Feldman, J. Chrobak, Z. Liberek and J. Szajewski, 'Four Cases of Poisoning with the Extract of Yew (*Taxus baccata*) Needles', *Polskie Archiwum Medycyny Wewnetrznej*, 79/1, (1988), pp. 26–9.

3 A. Dumitru, 'Die Eibe (*Taxus baccata* L.): Eine Botanisch-ökologische Sowie Medizinische und Kulturhistorische Betrachtung', diploma in Forest Science (Munich, 1992), p. 103.

4 H. Osthoff, 'Wie Giftig ist die Eibe (*Taxus baccata* L.)?', *Der Eibenfreund*, 15 (Markgroeningen, 2009), pp. 214–18.

5 P. A. Thomas and A. Polwart, 'Biological Flora of the British Isles. *Taxus baccata* L.', *Journal of Ecology*, 91 (2003), p. 506.

6 Personal communication with Prof. L. Paule, Faculty of Forestry, Zvolen, Slovakia.

7 Thomas, 'Biological Flora of the British Isles'; H. Osthoff, 'Medizin aus der Eibe', *Der Eibenfreund*, 8 (Markgroeningen, 2001), pp. 70–75.

8 Thomas, 'Biological Flora of the British Isles', p. 506.
9 9 g of leaves was used to base the ruling in a court case in Germany: Administrative Court, case 5K 268/07 from 14 November 2007, and Higher Administrative Court, case 8A 90/08 from January 2008 (Osthoff 2009).
10 Osthoff, 'Wie Giftig ist die Eibe', pp. 214–18.
11 Arthur Hort, trans., *Theophrastus: Enquiry into Plants*, III, X, 2 (Cambridge, MA, and London, 1916).
12 In Dumitru, 'Die Eibe (*Taxus baccata* L.)', p. 100.
13 Pliny, *The Natural History*, XVI, 20.
14 Dioscurides cited in D. Voliotis, 'Historical and Environmental Significance of the Yew (*T. b. L.*)', *Israel Journal of Botany*, 35 (1986), pp. 47–52.
15 Kukowka in Dumitru, 'Die Eibe (*Taxus baccata* L.)', p. 96.
16 Narayan P. Manandhar, *Plants and People of Nepal* (Portland, OR, 2002); H. Osthoff, 'Medizin aus der Eibe', *Der Eibenfreund*, 8 (Markgroeningen, 2001), p. 72; D. Brandis, *Illustrations of the Forest Flora of North-west and Central India* (London, 1874), in John Lowe, *The Yew-trees of Great Britain and Ireland* (London, 1897), p. 139.
17 Daniel E. Moerman, *Native American Ethnobotany* (Portland, OR, 1998), pp. 551–3; Hal Jr Hartzell, *The Yew Tree: A Thousand Whispers* (Eugene, OR, 1991), pp. 136, 139.
18 Dumitru, 'Die Eibe (*Taxus baccata* L.)', p. 105; Osthoff, 'Medizin aus der Eibe', pp. 70–75.
19 W. J. Gradishar et al., 'Phase III Trial of Nanoparticle Albumin-bound Paclitaxel Compared with Polyethylated Castor Oil-based Paclitaxel in Women with Breast Cancer', *Journal of Clinical Oncology*, 23/31 (2005), pp. 7794–803.

7 Political Yew

1 Robert Hardy, *Longbow: A Social and Military History* (Sparkford, 1992), p. 17.
2 Ibid., p. 30; Thomas Scheeder, 'Zur Anthropogenen Nutzung der Eibe (*Taxus baccata* L.)', *Der Eibenfreund*, 7 (Markgroeningen, 2000), p. 68.
3 Robert Hardy, 'Longbow', *Living History*, August 2004, pp. 14–19. See also www.maryrose.org.
4 Hardy, *Longbow: A Social and Military History*; Hardy, 'Longbow', p. 18. King Edward I's decree: John Lowe, *The Yew-trees of Great Britain and Ireland* (London, 1897), pp. 118–19.
5 Hardy, *Longbow: A Social and Military History*, pp. 49–50.
6 Quoted in Hal Jr Hartzell, *The Yew Tree: A Thousand Whispers* (Eugene, OR, 1991), p. 39.
7 *Encyclopedia Britannica* 2004; Anne Curry, *Agincourt: A New History* (Stroud, 2005).
8 Hardy, *Longbow: A Social and Military History*; Scheeder, 'Zur Anthropogenen Nutzung der Eibe', p. 72. For the life and work methods of bowyers see

M. Strickland and Robert Hardy, *The Great Warbow: From Hastings to the Mary Rose* (Stroud, 2005), pp. 20–25.

9 Ibid., p. 42.

10 Fred Hageneder, *Yew: A History* (Stroud, 2007), chap. 24; Thomas Scheeder, *Die Eibe (Taxus baccata L.): Hoffnung Für ein Fast Verschwundenes Waldvolk* (Eching, 1994), pp. 43–6; Scheeder, 'Zur Anthropogenen Nutzung der Eibe', p. 72; Christian Küchli, *Auf den Eichen Wachsen die Besten Schinken: Zehn intime Baumporträts* (Zürich, 1987).

11 G. Mutschlechner and O. Kostenzer, 'Zur Natur- und Kulturgeschichte der Eibe in Nordtirol', *Veröffentl. des Tiroler Landesmuseums Ferdinandeum*, 53 (1973), pp. 277–8.

12 Scheeder, 'Zur Anthropogenen Nutzung der Eibe', p. 75; John Lowe, *The Yew-trees of Great Britain and Ireland* (London, 1897), pp. 104–5.

13 Ibid., p. 125; Scheeder, 'Zur Anthropogenen Nutzung der Eibe', p. 80.

8 Aesthetic Yew

1 Quoted in Jean-Luc Bouvet and Francois-Xavier Vives, *Plant Secrets: The Yew – Beneficial Poison*, film documentary (Paris, 2010).

2 Eike Jablonski, 'Die Bedeutung der Fibe im Gartenbau', *Der Eibenfreund*, 8 (Markgroeningen, 2001), pp. 60–69; Siegfried Sommer, 'Die Eibe in der Lanschaftsarchitektur: Früher und Heute', *Der Eibenfreund*, 5 (Markgroeningen, 1998), pp. 17–22.

3 Roddy Llewellyn, 'Genius with a Wild Streak: William Robinson "Invented" Modern Gardening', *Mail on Sunday* (London, 30 March 1997), p. 61.

4 Fred Hageneder, *Yew: A History* (Stroud, 2007), p. 116. Gravetye Manor is now a luxury hotel (www.gravetyemanor.co.uk).

5 Jablonski, 'Die Bedeutung der Eibe im Gartenbau', pp. 60–69.

6 Hageneder, *Yew*, p. 205.

7 H. Baumann, *Die griechische Pflanzenwelt in Mythos, Kunst und Literatur* (Munich, 1999), p. 37, after Pausanias.

8 Hayrettin Kayacik and Burhan Aytug, *Gordion Kral Mezari'nin Agac Malzemesi Üzerinde Ormancilik Yönünden Arastirmalar* (Istanbul, 1968); Russell Meiggs, *Trees and Timber in the Ancient Mediterranean World* (Oxford, 1982).

9 Hageneder, *Yew*, p. 230.

10 Thomas Scheeder, *Die Eibe (Taxus baccata L.): Hoffnung Für ein Fast Verschwundenes Waldvolk* (Eching, 1994), p. 50 f; A. Dumitru, 'Die Eibe (*Taxus baccata* L.): Eine Botanisch-ökologische Sowie Medizinische und Kulturhistorische Betrachtung', diploma in Forest Science (Munich, 1992), pp. 122–5.

11 Ibid., p. 124.

12 Karlo Amirgulashvili and Tamar Nadiradze, 'Die Eibe in Georgien, Insbesondere in der Bazara-Schlucht', *Der Eibenfreund*, 16 (Markgroeningen, 2010), pp. 84–93.

13 Both quoted in Hal Jr Hartzell, *The Yew Tree: A Thousand Whispers* (Eugene, OR, 1991), pp. 243–79.

14 Wordsworth's 'Yew-trees', quoted in Fred Hageneder, *Yew: A History*, p. 121. See also Peter Ackroyd, 'The Poets Who Built the Modern World', *The Times* (London, 14 January 2006), pp. 12–13.

15 'Ash Wednesday', section IV.

16 My translation of 'Man sagt, dass Schlaf, ein schlimmer, Dir aus den Nadeln raucht – Ach! wacher war ich nimmer, Als rings von dir umhaucht.' Quoted in Dumitru, 'Die Eibe (*Taxus baccata* L.)', p. 95.

17 Personal communication with A. Meredith. See also Geoff Chapman and Bob Young, *Box Hill* (Lyme Regis, 1979), p. 127; Janet Dunbar, *J. M. Barrie: The Man Behind the Image* (London, 1970), pp. 64, 168; Anand Chetan and Diana Brueton, *The Sacred Yew* (London, 1994), p. 171.

18 'To Minnie', *A Child's Garden of Verses*, 1885, quoted in D. Rodger, J. Stokes and J. Ogilvie, *Heritage Trees of Scotland* (London, 2003).

19 Fontane [1873], quoted in A. Brande, 'Die Eibe in Berlin Einst und Jetzt', *Der Eibenfreund*, 8 (Markgroeningen, 2001), pp. 24–43.

20 A. Desmond and J. Moore, *Darwin* (London, 1991), p. 357.

21 Anand Chetan and Diana Brueton, *The Sacred Yew* (London, 1994), p. 194.

22 Dumitru, 'Die Eibe (*Taxus baccata* L.)', p. 133, after B. Quantz, 'Eibenschutz in Hannover und Thüringen vor 70–75 Jahren', *Naturschutz*, 18/4 (1937), pp. 76–9.

23 The Staatliche Stelle für Naturdenkmalpflege in Preussen was founded in 1906 at Gdansk, and moved to Berlin in 1911 (Thomas Scheeder and A. Brande, 'Die Bedeutung der Eibenforschung von Hugo Conwentz für die Geschichte des Naturschutzes', *Arch. für Nat.-Lands.*, 36 (1997), pp. 295–304).

24 Quote from the parish magazine, 1880, in Anand Chetan and Diana Brueton, *The Sacred Yew* (London, 1994), pp. 243–4.

25 Brande, 'Die Eibe in Berlin Einst und Jetzt', pp. 24–43.

26 Scheeder, *Die Eibe* (Taxus baccata L.)', pp. 53–65.

9 Metaphysical Yew

1 George Henslow, *Plants of the Bible* (London, 1906), p. 51, n. 2.

2 Jacob Grimm and Wilhelm Grimm, *Deutsches Wörterbuch: Elektronische Ausgabe der Erstbearbeitung* (Frankfurt a.M., 2004).

3 Ivanov (*Problemy Indoevropejskogo Jazykoznanija*), in Jaan Puhvel, *Hittite Etymological Dictionary*, vols I–II (Berlin, New York and Amsterdam, 1984).

4 *Encyclopedia Britannica* (2004); Marieluise Deissmann, ed. and trans., *Caesar: De bello Gallico/Der Gallische Krieg* (Stuttgart, 1980).

5 Georgia: personal communication with Prof. M. Pridnya, September 2005. Verified with K. Amirgulashvili in 2011. Ainu: M. Kawase, 'Japanese Yew (*Taxus cuspidata*)', *Proceedings of the International Taxus Symposium*, *Horticulture Series*, 421 (1975), A1–A5.

6   Volkert Haas, *Magie und Mythen im Reich der Hethiter,* vol. 1 (Hamburg, 1977), pp. 11–14; H. A. Hoffner Jr, *Hittite Myths* (Atlanta, GA, 1998), p. 11. Quote from KUB [Keilschrift-Urkunden aus Boghazköy], XXIX 1 IV 17–20, in Puhvel, *Hittite Etymological Dictionary.*

7   KUB [Keilschrift-Urkunden aus Boghazköy], XXIX A 27–35, in H. A. Hoffner Jr, *Hittite Myths* (Atlanta, GA, 1998), p. 18. For sheepskins compare Haas, *Magie und Mythen im Reich der Hethiter,* p. 153.

8   Pindar, *Pythian* IV, in C. M. Bowra, trans., *Pindar: The Odes* (London, 1969); Apollodorus 1.3, in Robin Hard, trans., *Apollodorus: The Library of Greek Mythology* (Oxford, 1997). Compare the Golden Lamb of Atreus in Arthur B. Cook, *Zeus: A Study in Ancient Religion,* vol. 1 (Cambridge, 1914), pp. 405–9.

9   Apollonius, IV, 1132, in Hilda M. Ransome, *The Sacred Bee in Ancient Times and Folklore* (London, 1937), p. 101; Robert Graves, *The Greek Myths,* vols 1–11 (Harmondsworth, 1955), 144.b.

10   R. Hunter, trans., Apollonius of Rhodes, *Jason and the Golden Fleece (The Argonautica)* (Oxford, 1998), pp. 102–3.

11   Haas, *Magie und Mythen im Reich der Hethiter,* p. 118.

12   W. Helbig, *Das Homerische Epos aus den Denkmälern Erläutert* (Leipzig, 1887), p. 440, in Arthur B. Cook, *Zeus: A Study in Ancient Religion,* vol. 111 (Cambridge, 1940), p. 364. Also compare p. 367.

13   Pytheas, Diodorus Siculus, Strabo, in Barry Cunliffe, *The Extraordinary Voyage of Pytheas the Greek* (New York, 2002), pp. 94, 106.

14   Joseph Campbell, *The Masks of God: Occidental Mythology* (New York, 1964), p. 301; Fred Hageneder, *The Spirit of Trees: Science, Synthesis and Inspiration* (Edinburgh and New York, 2000), p. 232; Michael Dames, *Mythic Ireland* (London, 1996), pp. 62, 77, 80; Françoise le Roux and Christian-J. Guyonvarch, *Die Druiden* (Engerda, 1996), pp. 500–501.

15   Joseph Campbell, *The Masks of God: Occidental Mythology* (New York, 1964), p. 31.

16   Hilda E. Davidson, *Roles of the Northern Goddess* (London and New York, 1998), pp. 8–10, 182.

17   Ursula Dronke, *The Poetic Edda,* vol. 11: *Mythological Poems* (Oxford, 1997), p. 44.

18   Hilda E. Davidson, *The Lost Beliefs of Northern Europe* (London and New York, 1993), p. 73.

19   Arthur B. Cook, *Zeus: A Study in Ancient Religion,* vol. 111 (Cambridge, 1940), p. 180; Pausanias X, 12, 4: 'overgrown places used to be called Idai', in Peter Levi, trans., *Pausanias: Guide to Greece,* vols I & 11 (London, 1979).

20   A. Dumitru, 'Die Eibe (*Taxus baccata* L.): Eine Botanisch-ökologische Sowie Medizinische und Kulturhistorische Betrachtung', diploma in Forest Science (Munich, 1992), p. 93.

21   Völ. 7, 2; 57, 2. 'Yew Valley' in Thomas Scheeder, *Die Eibe* (Taxus baccata L.): *Hoffnung für ein fast verschwundenes Waldvolk* (Eching, 1994), p. 7.

22   Hittite: KUB [Keilschrift-Urkunden aus Boghazköy], XII 20. 9, in Puhvel, *Hittite Etymological Dictionary*; Volsung saga: Arthur B. Cook, *Zeus:*

A Study in Ancient Religion, vol. II (Cambridge, 1925), p. 682; Ireland: *Dindsenchas* III, 'Mag Mugna', in Edward Gwynn, ed., *The Metrical Dindsenchas*, vols I–V (Dublin, 1903–35).

23 Quote from KBO [Keilschrift-Texte aus Boghazköy], VI 2 II 62, in Puhvel, *Hittite Etymological Dictionary*, 1984. Apulunuas inscriptions found on four Hittite altars, translated by Hrozny in 1936, in W.K.C. Guthrie, *The Greeks and their Gods* (London, 1950/1962), p. 86.

24 Guthrie, *The Greeks and their Gods*, p. 87.

25 Mircea Eliade, *A History of Religious Ideas: From the Stone Age to the Eleusinian Mysteries*, vol. I (Chicago, IL, 1978), p. 268.

26 Marcel de Cleene and Marie Claire Lejeune, *Compendium of Symbolic and Ritual Plants in Europe*, vol. I: *Trees and Shrubs* (Ghent, 2003), p. 742.

27 J. H. Mozley, trans., *Valerius Flaccus: Argonautica*, 1.730 (Cambridge, MA, and London, 1998).

28 Graves, *The Greek Myths*, 18.3.

29 Marcel de Cleene and Marie Claire Lejeune, *Compendium of Symbolic and Ritual Plants in Europe, vol. I, Trees and Shrubs*, Ghent 2003, pp. 741–2.

30 Fred Hageneder, *Yew: A History* (Stroud, 2007), chap. 31.

31 Pausanias mentions Olympia, Megalopolis, Messene and Tegea.

32 Fred Hageneder, *The Living Wisdom of Trees: Natural History, Folklore, Symbolism, Healing* (London, 2005), published in the US as *The Meanings of Trees* (San Francisco, CA, 2005), pp. 100–101.

33 Russell Meiggs, *Trees and Timber in the Ancient Mediterranean World* (Oxford, 1982), pp. 24–5.

34 W.H.S. Jones, trans., *Pliny: Natural History* (London, 1960), 16.8.

35 Hageneder, *Yew*, pp. 145–6.

36 Ibid., chap. 30, for full discussion.

37 A. D. Melville, trans., *Ovid: Metamorphoses* (Oxford, 1986), VIII, 743–5, 758–62.

38 Theophrastus, III. X. 2: 'The yew [*milos*] has also but one kind, is straightgrowing, grows readily, and is like the silver-fir [*elate*], except that it is not so tall and is more branched.' (Fir, *Abies alba*, can reach 60 m in height.) Dioscurides, *De materia medica*: 'It is a tree resembling the fir as regards the leaves and the size, it grows in Italy and Narvonia of Spain.' (Cited in Voliotis 1986, p. 47.) Also possibly Strabo, *Geographica*, IV, 202, about Liguria: 'with trees so large that the diameter of their thickness is sometimes found to be eight feet'. Dumitru, 'Die Eibe (*Taxus baccata* L.)'.

39 Monika Hellmund, 'Geböttcherte Eibenholzeimer aus der Römischen Kaiserzeit: Funde von Gommern, Ldkr. Jerichower Land, Sachsen–Anhalt', *Der Eibenfreund*, 12 (Markgroeningen, 2005), pp. 157–64; Hageneder, *Yew*, p. 219–20

40 Dronke, *The Poetic Edda*, p. 107.

41 Ibid., p. 109. Also in *Gylfaginning*, in Ulf Diederichs, ed., *Germanische Götterlehre: Nach den Quellen der Lieder und der Prosa-Edda (tr. Felix Genzmer & Gustav Neckel)* (Cologne, 1984), p. 144.

42 Bryony Coles, 'Wood Species for Wooden Figures: A Glimpse of a Pattern', in Alex Gibson and Derek Simpson, eds, *Prehistoric Ritual and Religion* (Stroud, 1998), pp. 163–73; Hageneder, *Yew*, chap. 41.

43 *Forspjallsljóð*, stanza 1, quoted in Dronke, *The Poetic Edda*, p. 110.

44 R. Doht, *Der Rauschtrank im Germanischen Mythos*, Wiener Arbeiten z. Germanischen Altertumskunde und Philologie, 3 (Vienna 1974), pp. 30, 154, referring to Adam of Bremen.

45 Dumitru, 'Die Eibe (*Taxus baccata* L.)', p. 92.

10 Sacred Yew

1 C. Scott Littleton, *Understanding Shinto: Origins, Beliefs, Practices, Festivals, Spirits, Sacred Places* (London, 2002). Also personal communication with Chris Worrall.

2 Anand Chetan and Diana Brueton, *The Sacred Yew* (London, 1994), pp. 53, 218. Also Fred Hageneder, *The Heritage of Trees: History, Culture and Symbolism* (Edinburgh, 2001), p. 140.

3 Quoted in R. Bevan-Jones, *The Ancient Yew* (Bollington, 2002), p. 62.

4 John Lowe, *The Yew-trees of Great Britain and Ireland* (London, 1897), pp. 99–100, after John Evelyn's *Sylva* (1664), Nichol's *Extracts from Church-warden's Accounts* (1797), Brady's *Clavis Calendaria*.

5 *Encyclopedia Britannica* 2004.

6 Fred Hageneder, *The Spirit of Trees: Science, Synthesis and Inspiration* (Edinburgh and New York, 2000), p. 142, after Jonathan C. Davies, *Folk-Lore of West and Mid-Wales* (Aberystwyth, 1911), p. 55.

7 German original: *Unter Eiben kann kein Zauber bleiben.*

8 Helen Nicholson, *The Knights Templar: A New History* (Stroud, 2001), pp. 142–4.

9 Ean Begg, *The Cult of the Black Virgin* (London, 1996), pp. 16–102.

10 Barry Cunliffe, *The Extraordinary Voyage of Pytheas the Greek* (New York, 2002), pp. 4–5. Also personal communication with, and various (French) articles by, Christian Vaquier, the forestry warden of Ste Baume, in 2005.

11 Martin Palmer, Jay Ramsay and Kwok Man-Ho, *Kuan Yin: Myths and Prophecies of the Chinese Goddess of Compassion* (London and San Francisco, CA, 1995).

11 Threatened Yew

1 Hal Jr Hartzell, *The Yew Tree: A Thousand Whispers* (Eugene, OR, 1991); J. Goodman and V. Walsh, *The Story of Taxol: Nature and Politics in the Pursuit of an Anti-cancer Drug* (Cambridge, 2001), p. 87.

2 Ibid., p. 56. See also N. Vidensek et al., 'Taxol Content in Bark, Wood, Root, Leaf, Twig, and Seedling from Several *Taxus* Species', *Journal of Natural Products*, LIII/6 (1990), pp. 1609–10.

3 Goodman, *The Story of Taxol*, pp. 51, 54–61, 131, 208, 229–30.

4 Jerry F. Franklin et al., 'Ecological Characteristics of Old-growth Douglas-fir Forests', USDA (Forest Service): *General Technical Report*, PNW-118 (Portland, OR, 1981).

5 American TV news footage, in Jean-Luc Bouvet and Francois-Xavier Vives, *Plant Secrets: The Yew – Beneficial Poison*, film documentary (Paris, 2010).

6 Kingley Vale: personal communication with Richard Williamson. Conwentz: Thomas Scheeder and A. Brande, 'Die Bedeutung der Eibenforschung von Hugo Conwentz für die Geschichte des Naturschutzes', *Arch. für Nat.-Lands.*, 36 (1997), pp. 295–304.

7 Goodman, *The Story of Taxol*, p. 1; M. J. Shemluck et al., 'A Preliminary Study of the Taxane Chemistry and Natural History of the Mexican Yew, *Taxus globosa* Schltdl.', *Boletín de la Sociedad Botánica de México*, 72 (2003), pp. 119–27.

8 Stanley Scher, 'Weltweite Eibenvorkommen (*Taxus*) Neu Betrachtet', *Der Eibenfreund*, 6 (Markgroeningen, 2000), pp. 109–18, after World Conservation and Monitoring Centre (WCMC, www.wcmc.org.uk) 1999: Tree Conservation Database; WWF 1998; K. S. Walter and H. J. Gillitt, eds, IUCN *Red List of Threatened Plants* (Gland, 1997).

9 Scher, 'Weltweite Eibenvorkommen (*Taxus*) Neu Betrachtet', pp. 109–18.

10 Bouvet, *Plant Secrets: The Yew – Beneficial Poison*.

11 Emmanuelle Neyroumande, WWF, Paris, France, in Bouvet, *Plant Secrets: The Yew – Beneficial Poison*.

12 Ibid.

13 Ibid.

14 Personal communication with US forester and yew nurseryman David Pilz. See also Hartzell, *The Yew Tree: A Thousand Whispers*, pp. 198–9.

15 Scher, 'Weltweite Eibenvorkommen (*Taxus*) Neu Betrachtet', pp. 109–18, after K. S. Walter and H. J. Gillitt, eds, IUCN *Red List of Threatened Plants* (Gland, 1997). See also World Conservation and Monitoring Centre (WCMS), www.unep-wcmc.org.

16 Ibid.

17 Personal communication with Prof. Bartolomeo Schirone, Department of Agriculture, Forests, Nature and Energy (DAFNE), University of Tuscia, Viterbo, Italy.

18 Personal communication with Xavier G. Martí, president of the Amigos del Tejo, and ecologists at the forestry faculty in Madrid.

19 See 'Paterzeller Eibenwald', http://de.wikipedia.org.

20 Gregor Bozic and Hojka Kraigher, 'Current State of English Yew (*Taxus baccata* L.) Gene-Pool in Slovenia', *Der Eibenfreund*, 16 (Markgroeningen, 2010), pp. 40–44.

21 Hajri Haska, 'Some Data for Albania and Its Forests, Including *Taxus baccata*', *Der Eibenfreund*, 16 (Markgroeningen, 2010), pp. 45–9.

22 Seyed-Mohammad Waez Mousavi and Mohammad Maghsoudlou Nezhad, 'Yew (*Taxus baccata* L.) Population in Tuskaestan Valley, North Iran', *Der Eibenfreund*, 17 (Markgroeningen, 2011), pp. 147–51.

23 Hageneder, *Yew*.
24 Karlo Amirgulashvili and Tamar Nadiradze, 'Die Eibe in Georgien, Insbesondere in der Bazara-Schlucht', *Der Eibenfreund*, 16 (Markgroeningen, 2010), pp. 84–93; Karlo Amirgulashvili, Iosebi (Soso) Turashvili and Tamar Nadiradze, 'Die Eibe (*Taxus baccata* L.) in Georgien, Insbesondere in der Bazara- und Ilto-Schlucht', *Der Eibenfreund*, 17 (Markgroeningen, 2011), pp. 137–46. Also personal communication with the author.
25 Mikhail Pridnya, 'Pflanzensoziologische Stellung und Struktur des Chosta-Eibenvorkommens im West-Kaukasus Biosphärenreservat', *Der Eibenfreund*, 7 (Markgroeningen, 2000), pp. 22–7; Mikhail Pridnya, 'Eibenvorkommen im Kaukasus', *Der Eibenfreund*, 7 (Markgroeningen, 2000), pp. 28–9. Also personal communication with K. Amirgulashvili and Prof. Pridnya.
26 Food and Agriculture Organization of the United Nations, Global Forest Resources Assessment 2010, www.fao.org.
27 Quoted in Fred Hageneder, *The Heritage of Trees: History, Culture and Symbolism* (Edinburgh, 2001), p. 37.

Further Reading

Balog, James, *Tree: A New Vision of the American Forest* (New York, 2004)
   A massive volume that does the ancient tree giants justice, from a
   courageous pioneer in landscape photography
Cleene, Marcel de, and Marie Claire Lejeune, *Compendium of Symbolic and Ritual
   Plants in Europe*, vol. 1: *Trees and Shrubs* (Ghent, 2003)
   An excellent scholarly encyclopedia of trees in cultural history
Hageneder, Fred, *Yew: A History* (Stroud, 2011)
   A comprehensive in-depth study of the natural and cultural history of the
   yew tree, with colour photography throughout
Johnson, Owen, *Champion Trees of Britain and Ireland* (Richmond, 2011)
   Find the most venerable trees in your neighbourhood – or any locality
Kovalainen, Ritva, and Sanni Seppo, *Tree People* (Finland, 2006)
   Artistic, touching and completely unique! (check www.puidenkansa.net)
Lovric, Michelle, *The Forests: A Celebration of Nature in Word and Image*
   (Philadelphia and London, 1996)
   A touching collection of excerpts from time-honoured tree poetry and
   paintings
Miles, Archie, *Silva: The Tree in Britain* (London, 1999)
   A modern classic by the distinguished landscape photographer and
   researcher Archie Miles
Mitchell, Alan, *Alan Mitchell's Trees of Britain* (London, 1996)
   The leading expert on trees discusses the origin of over 150 species of
   British trees
Parker, Edward, and Anna Lewington, *Ancient Trees: Trees That Live for a Thousand
   Years* (London, 2012)
   A glorious celebration of some of the oldest trees in the world, with
   stunning photography by leading tree photographer Edward Parker and
   highly informative text
Robbins, Jim, *The Man Who Planted Trees: Lost Groves, Champion Trees and an Urgent
   Plan to Save the Planet* (New York, 2012)

Associations and Websites

ANCIENT YEW GROUP
www.ancient-yew.org

THE MEANING OF TREES
www.themeaningoftrees.com

THE WOODLAND TRUST (WT) AND THE ANCIENT TREE FORUM
www.woodland-trust.org.uk
www.ancient-tree-hunt.org.uk

THE TREE REGISTER (OF THE BRITISH ISLES)
www.treeregister.org

THE CONSERVATION FOUNDATION
www.conservationfoundation.co.uk

CARING FOR GOD'S ACRE
www.caringforgodsacre.org.uk

Acknowledgements

Most heartfelt thanks, first of all, to my partner Elaine Vijaya, for once again supporting my tree commitments. Many thanks to all who researched yew before me, especially my colleagues at the AYG, Paul Greenwood, Tim Hills, Toby Hindson and Andy McGeeney, and members of the German Yew Society, *Eibenfreunde*, particularly Dr Thomas Scheeder, Hubert Rössner and Christian Wolf. Without their support this book would not have been possible. For their professional support I deeply thank, most of all, Prof. Bartolomeo Schirone and his team at the University of Tuscía, Viterbo (Italy); Dr Ulrich Pietzarka, Saxonian State Arboretum, Tharandt (Germany); Prof. Ladislav Paule, Faculty of Forestry, Zvolen (Slovakia) and Dr Arthur Brande, Ecological Institute at the Technical University of Berlin. Very special thanks to Chris Worrall (England), Xavier García Martí (Spain), Dr David Pilz (USA), Dr Necmi Aksoy (Turkey) and Dr Stanley Scher (USA). I would also like to thank all the photographers and artists who contributed their stunning work to this unique book, the editing and production teams – and of course you, the reader.

Photo Acknowledgements

The author and the publishers wish to express their thanks to the below sources of illustrative material and/or permission to reproduce it.

Ignacio Abella: pp. 6, 60, 143 top; Carlos Amirgulashvili: pp.177, 178, 180; Christopher Cornwell: pp. 32, 118 bottom, 119, 148; Frank Depoix: pp. 36, 50; Hans Diebschlag: p. 120; Thaw Collection, Fenimore Art Museum, Cooperstown, New York: p. 15; Paul Greenwood: pp. 10, 31; Tim Hills: pp. 9, 29, 51, 52, 55, 56, 57 top right and left, 72 bottom, 73, 94, 137, 160, 179; Fred Hageneder: pp. 11, 22, 38 top, 53, 61, 65, 69, 72 top, 74, 75, 109, 112, 117, 131, 136, 138, 140, 141, 142, 143 bottom, 149, 152, 156, 176; Ben Lovegrove: p. 146; Shaun McDonagh: pp. 86 bottom, 91; Andy McGeeney: pp. 27, 57 bottom, 77, 83, 155, 165; NASA: pp. 22, 109; Peter Norton: p. 157; Edward Parker: pp. 24–5, 45–6; Christine Redgate: pp. 86 top, 87 top right; Gerd Rossen: p. 87 top left; Antonello Salis: pp. 38 centre, 95; Shutterstock: pp. 115 (kirych), 116 (Jose Ignacio Soto); Swedish Museum of Natural History: pp. 17, 19; F. Taddei/B. Schirone: p. 35; Chris Worrall: pp. 41, 132, 133, 134, 153, 154, 174, 175; Christian Wolf: pp. 34, 42, 43, 44, 79, 135.

Index